T0392277

THE
PASTOR'S PEN

*A Weekly Devotional for an
In-Depth Bible Study*

PASTOR RICHIE THOMAS

WESTBOW
PRESS®
A DIVISION OF THOMAS NELSON
& ZONDERVAN

WestBow Press books may be ordered through booksellers or by contacting:

WestBow Press
A Division of Thomas Nelson & Zondervan
1663 Liberty Drive
Bloomington, IN 47403
www.westbowpress.com
844-714-3454

King James Version Scriptures marked KJV are taken
from the King James Version, public domain.

ISBN: 979-8-3850-3239-6 (sc)
ISBN: 979-8-3850-3240-2 (e)

Library of Congress Control Number: 2024918287

Print information available on the last page.

WestBow Press rev. date: 10/21/2024

This book is dedicated to my dear friend and mentor, the late Howard Cox (1941-2023), Pastor of Word of Faith Bible Church from 1991 to 2023.

The Apostle Paul wrote in 1 Corinthians 15:10 (King James Bible, 1611), "But by the grace of God I am what I am…". I echo this statement, for I know that I am who He has called me to be by His grace alone. However, God has used many people to steer me in the correct direction in order to walk in the righteousness of Christ in Truth and to answer His call. Pastor Howard Cox was the single most influential spiritual guidance counselor I have had in my life. He was my pastor, my mentor, and my friend. I am grateful that God placed Brother Howard in my life and can only pray that I may have the influence and impact on others that Howard had on me for Christ's sake.

I would also like to thank my beautiful and supportive wife, Sara, for standing by me and encouraging me when others fled. She has been the perfect mother to our children and help meet for me, and I give thanks unto God for her in my life. And I would also like to thank my church family, the wonderful congregation at Word of Faith Bible Church in Crescent City, Florida. Thank you for entrusting me as the shepherd of this flock that God has called me to. We are truly the body of Christ and are a family. The love that exists in our family is an encouragement to me as well as to the visitors of our church. And as with any family, there are times when we must all be reproved and rebuked as well as exhorted, as the Bible tells us in 2 Timothy 4:2. I am thankful that we are mature enough in the Lord to understand that and come back to continue to worship together, even when our toes might get stepped on from time to time. My prayer is that the churches all over God's creation would be mature enough to receive this as well.

CONTENTS

INTRODUCTION

The following work is a collection of articles that I wrote for our local paper, *The Putnam County Courier Journal* between 2019 and 2021. Unfortunately, the paper is no longer in existence. However, over time several people have asked me about the articles, so I decided to publish them as a collection. This devotional is comprised of 52 articles including the first one which was written specifically for this book. You can read one article each week, along with the corresponding scripture, and pray about it, seeking God's wisdom by the power of His Holy Spirit. Revisit the devotional each day of the week as you continue to pray and journal your experiences and spiritual growth.

Some articles may ruffle the feathers and be offensive to readers because they deal with hard topics. You may not agree with me on every point that I am trying to make. All I ask is that you be as the Bereans in Acts chapter 17 and study the scriptures for yourself. Believe, not because of what I have written. Believe because it is what is written in God's Holy Word. All Christians should study to show ourselves approved unto God and apply the Wisdom of His Word to our lives daily. I pray that this work may aid you in your walk with the Lord and help you draw closer to Him. If it is a blessing in your life, then I encourage you to share it with others.

Remember, as believers in Christ Jesus, the saved should be telling others about the Saving Grace of God through faith in Jesus Christ and His finished works of the death, burial, and resurrection. Without this faith, humanity is doomed. Christ came to die for the world (see John 3:16), so those of us who are saved, should be helping to lead others to this decision in their lives by their own free-will. We are not saved to be silent. We are saved to tell others so they too can be saved. And those of us who are saved should spend time with the Lord daily in prayer and the study of His Word while applying His Word to our daily living. We should grow in our relationship with the Lord, becoming more like Him and less like our old self. We are ambassadors for Christ and others are watching. If we don't live the Bible, how can we expect others to believe it? The trumpet is getting ready to sound, and the voice of the archangel is about to be heard. Let us all do our part while there is still time to do so.

Thank you for purchasing this book. I am honored and humbled that you would do so. In this economy, I know how difficult it is to spend money on anything other than necessities. I gratefully appreciate the fact that you chose to buy this devotional. But be warned, it will make you think and study the Bible. I pray it is a blessing to you and that you are fully surrendered to the Lord. May God bless you to bless others, and continue to use you for His Glory, Honor and Praise!

THE TRUTH SHALL MAKE YOU FREE

I am quite alarmed at how many people who profess to be Christians that still follow after worldly lusts. These lusts have crept their way into our churches across the nation and the world for that matter. There really isn't any difference between the church today and the world. They have dropped their denominational names such as Baptist, Methodist and Lutheran in favor of some cool, hip and catchy phrases. I am not attacking the people that attend these Churches necessarily, but more of the leadership. Why? Because one of two things is happening. Either they do not know any better, or they do and do not care. Either way it is not a good thing to do. But just what is the problem that I am alluding to?

Modernism is the problem. Modernists have replaced the truth with a lie and entice their congregation with attractions rather than the truth of the Word of God. The music is worldly, and the attire of the pastor is worldly, therefore the attire of the congregation is worldly. Modesty, what is that? Church today looks like a carnival in appearance and function. It has been stated, "whatever you attract them with is what you have to keep them with". I mean no offense, but we should not be attracting congregations with pop music, games, ice-cream socials, sports and recreation, or any other form of entertainment. Charles Spurgeon once said, "If we are to see the church of God really restored to her pristine glory, we must have back this plain, simple, gospel-preaching" (Spurgeon, 2019). But that is just it. The pastors of these churches are not interested in restoring the church or feeding the flock with the truth. They want to tickle the ears and rub the backs of the congregants, making them feel good. This is so they will come back next week and put more money in the offering. Oh, what filthy lucre does to the wicked.

We need to get away from the world and its worldliness and get back to preaching the Bible. We need to be faithful unto God and His Holy Word. The Apostle Paul told Timothy, "Preach the word; be instant in season, out of season; reprove, rebuke, exhort with all longsuffering and doctrine" (2 Timothy 4:2). Some of these pastors have forgotten that. Or perhaps they never knew it, because they do not know God's Word at all. That is why it is absolutely imperative that the individual believer study his or her Bible for themselves, so they are not fooled by the soothsayers of the modern pulpit. Read it for yourselves, study it for yourselves. Pray and ask with all sincerity that God reveal to you, His Word. He will do it! You will be astonished at what you learn. Jesus said in John 8:32, "And ye shall know the truth, and the truth shall make you free." Study, pray, repeat the process daily, and be free in Christ Jesus.

- **Read 2 Timothy 4:1-8**
- Does your Church Preach the Word of God from the Scriptures?
- Or does your Church spend more time with entertainment and motivational speaking?
- Do you spend time daily in prayer and the study of the Bible?
- If not, I encourage you to spend some alone time with the Word of God. Perhaps begin by spending 15-30 minutes reading scripture and praying about what you have read.
  - o I begin with prayer, study His Word while also talking to The Lord during my study time, and taking notes. I then end with prayer.
  - o Ask God to reveal His understanding to you. He will.
- Make notes of the things that you learn from God's Word and journal them daily and compare them to what you have been told by others, including pastors, preachers, and Sunday school teachers.
  - o Does what you read and study match what they are preaching and teaching?

A DOOR OF HOPE

The Spanish-American Philosopher, George Santayana once famously said, "Those who cannot remember the past are condemned to repeat it". That could not be any truer for Americans today. This country was founded on Christian principles. Of the 56 signers of the Declaration of Independence, 51 of them were members of a Christian church (Koukol, 2013). That means that 91 percent of the signers of the Declaration of Independence were Christian men who were establishing our freedom as a nation. Many today try to debate the fact that we were established by Christians and upon Christian principles based on the Holy Bible. However, a quick study of our historical documents will reveal the intense belief in God and faith in Jesus. 248 years later we have fallen so far from where we once were as a nation. Where we were once firmly planted in Christianity, we have now gone the way of ancient Israel and followed other nations, rather than leading them. We have become enamored by the gods of our neighbors and have forgotten the way of the Lord.

If we study how God dealt with Israel in the past, we will know where we stand and where we are heading as a nation today in the United States. We continually seek after wickedness and then wonder why we aren't blessed or why we are facing hardships as a nation. God spoke through the prophet Hosea and said, "…Go, take unto thee a wife of whoredoms and children of whoredoms: for the land hath committed great whoredom, departing from the LORD" (Hosea 1:2). God told Israel they had departed from Him, just like we Americans have departed from Him today. We have forgotten the ways of our fathers and mothers and have gone our own way, whoring after whatever desires entice us. God pleaded with Israel in the ancient days, and he pleads with us today to put away our wickedness and return to our loving Father. God told Hosea, "Therefore, behold, I will hedge up thy way with thorns, and make a wall, that she shall not find her paths" (Hosea 2:6).

God delivers promises, not threats. However, our merciful and gracious Heavenly Father always provides a way back to Him, even when it seems that we are too far gone. In Hosea chapter 2, verses 14 and 15 God says that He will speak comfortably and give a door of hope unto Israel so that they will return to Him. He has also given a door of hope unto the world. Jesus says in John chapter 10 that He is the door of the sheep. "I am the door: by me if any man enter in, he shall be saved, and shall go in and out, and find pasture" (John 10:9). This goes for you and me as individuals and all of us as a people and a nation of Americans. If you are a born-again believer in Christ Jesus, then you have the promise of eternal life and blessings forever. That should be enough to make us all rejoice in the Lord and return our country unto God and His ways. Because we are His people, and He is our God.

- **Read Hosea Chapter 2**
- How does knowing that God dealt harshly with the Jews, His own chosen people, change your idea of who God is and how we are supposed to behave as Christians, who are also children of the Lord?
- Do you see how the modern world has departed from God and are not living righteously according to His Word?
  - o Just because the world does ungodly things does not mean we need to be partakers of those things.
  - o In fact, we should strive to live as righteous and holy people, separated unto God.
- **Read John Chapter 10:1-21**
- How does knowing that Jesus is the Good Shepherd and the One who laid down His life for the World, shape your view on how we should live?
- Even though we know we all come short of the glory of God (Romans 3:23), we should strive to live a mature life in Christ. Give God glory by living a holy and acceptable life unto Him.

LET BROTHERLY LOVE CONTINUE

Today more than ever, Christians are facing persecution. We see it in the Middle East, and even in other parts of the world where followers of Christ are being beaten, tortured, imprisoned, and even killed for their faith in Jesus Christ. Even in America we have people who are using their prejudices against Christianity to push believers out of mainstream society. Our own government has sought to remove the Bible, God, prayer, and any mention of Jesus from our schools, courthouses, and public places exclaiming "separation of church and state." It is indeed a slap in the face to all who believe and know that this country was founded on the very principals of the Bible and our forefathers' faith in Jesus.

However, we should all be reminded that our society is not rejecting us, they are rejecting Jesus. They rejected Him two thousand years ago, and they are still doing it today. Jesus knew it would happen and told us in the Bible, "Yea, and all that will live godly in Christ Jesus shall suffer persecution. But evil men and seducers shall wax worse and worse, deceiving, and being deceived" (2 Timothy 3:12-13). But I am also reminded of His Word to do good and not grow weary of doing so, even when we face the trials and tribulations in this life. The Apostle Paul tells us "But continue thou in the things which thou hast learned and hast been assured of, knowing of whom thou hast learned them; And that from a child thou hast known the holy scriptures, which are able to make thee wise unto salvation through faith which is in Christ Jesus" (2 Timothy 3:14-15).

Remember that we do good to others because Christ lives in us. We work and live for Jesus, not for man. Everything we do, should be for and about Christ. Therefore, we should never grow weary of doing good. Jesus said, "...Verily I say unto you, inasmuch as ye have done it unto one of the least of these my brethren, ye have done it unto me."

(Matthew 25:40). I know it can be hard sometimes and we often fail but let us all be renewed by the spirit daily and seek to do good unto others for the love of Christ. Regardless of how we are treated, let us place our faith in Jesus and do as He instructed us in His Holy Word and "Let brotherly love continue" (Hebrews 13:1).

- **Read Hebrews 13:1-3**
- How does knowing that God is involved in our everyday life, and sees everything we do, shape how you interact with others?
- Do you find it hard to demonstrate the love of Christ when others are not being so loving themselves?
- We all face persecution. Some more than others. How does facing persecution interfere with your Goldy living?
- I encourage you this week, to settle the scriptures in your heart, and strive to continue with brotherly love, even in the face of persecution and our daily trials and tribulations.
- **Read Matthew 25:40 again**.
- **Read Romans 14:8**
- Please keep this in mind, what we do, we do for the Lord because we are doing it as unto the Lord!
- Remember not just who you are, but whose you are.
- Pray for God to direct your steps in brotherly love.
- Journal your experiences and add any comments associated with this week's devotional.

TRUST, OBEY & BELIEVE

When Jesus was preparing for His triumphant entry into Jerusalem, he told two of his disciples to go into a village and loose a colt that they will find tied up that no one had ever ridden before. He also told them when a man asks why you are loosening the colt say "…that the Lord hath need of him, and straightway he will send him hither" (Mark 11:3). The two disciples without hesitation or worry or fear did as Jesus had directed. They found the colt, started untying him and were questioned as to why they were doing so. The scripture tells us, "And they said unto them even as Jesus had commanded: and they let him go (Mark 11:6). What a powerful lesson in trusting and obeying our Lord Jesus Christ.

We can be confident today that if we follow the Word of God and do as the Lord has commanded us to do, that things will turn out exactly as He has said they would. Nothing is by our own power or understanding but by the power of the Holy Spirit that the Lord has given to all who believe on the name of Jesus. Jesus continued in the book of Mark to instruct and guide the disciples by telling them to "have faith in God" (Mark 11:22). And then He gives one of the most powerful statements ever. Jesus says, "For verily I say unto you, That whosoever shall say unto this mountain, Be thou removed, and be thou cast into the sea: and shall not doubt in his heart, but shall believe that those things which he saith shall come to pass; he shall have whatsoever he saith" (Mark 11:23).

I wonder how many people professing Christianity really believe in their heart what Jesus has told us throughout His Word. Sometimes it seems as though people are merely going through the motions and saying all the right things, and maybe attending church a couple times a month or a few times a year to check the block but really don't fully trust and obey. Perhaps it is because some truly do not believe. I have heard many say that they prayed and did not get what they asked for and therefore their faith has waned. The Bible tells us, "Ye ask, and receive not, because ye ask amiss, that ye may consume it upon your lusts" (James 4:3). Many times, we ask God for things like he is Santa Claus and not the Lord, God Almighty. We ask for things to consume for our personal satisfaction without regard to pleasing the Lord and seeking His righteousness and His will for our lives. The disciples of Jesus did as He had asked, and all was as Jesus said it would be. We too are disciples of Jesus, followers of Christ. Let us trust in Him, believe what He has told us, and go forth and do what He has told us to do. Do it with confidence, knowing the outcome will be as He has instructed in His Word. Have faith in God and trust, obey, and believe.

- **Read Mark 11:1-11**
- How does the story of Jesus' triumphant entry into Jerusalem help you better understand obedience unto the Lord?
- When we know the Word of God is Truth, we can have confidence that it will be just as Jesus has said it will be.
- **Now Read Mark 11:12-14 & 20-26**
- Do you believe that you can tell a physical mountain to be moved and it will happen?
- In order to understand the answer, we must understand the will of God.
- He tells us whatever we ask for, if we believe it shall be done!
- However, we must ask according to God's Will.
- Is casting a mountain into the sea when we want it to happen really God's will?
- Or is it our own desire to show off?
- **Read James 4:3 again.**
- Too many times when we pray, we are seeking things for our own lusts (or fleshly satisfaction).
- Before I pray, I settle things in my heart regarding what I am about to speak with God about (He already knows this).
- I ask myself is this for God's glory, honor and praise, or for my personal fleshly desire.
- In the Lord's prayer, Jesus teaches us to pray by saying "thy will be done" speaking of God the Father's will (See Matthew 6:10).
- That is our template. That is how we should pray for all things. Not my will, but thine Lord.

THE HIDDEN GOSPEL?

In the book of Mark, Jesus tells us to "...Go ye into all the world, and preach the gospel to every creature. He that believeth and is baptized shall be saved; but he that believeth not shall be damned" (Mark 16:15-16). Our Lord has given us a command to preach the gospel to everybody. We should not be selective as to who we speak to about the saving grace of Jesus. We are supposed to tell everybody! Yet many of us only mention the name of Jesus on Sunday when we go to church. This should not be. We have the gift of eternal life burning in our hearts and it should be evident, not just on Sunday, but every day in our conversations and our actions. We should be eager to share the love, grace, and mercy of God to the people we meet with each and every day, not for our sakes but for their sakes and for the glory of the Lord!

I know the devil has worked diligently to make it hard for us to speak openly about God and His only begotten son Jesus. Satan has worked through the minds and thoughts of non-believers that are sitting in positions of authority to interfere with our ability to freely express the gospel of Jesus. That subtle serpent has continued to try to influence us that we should just keep Jesus to ourselves. But that is not what the Bible teaches us to do, Jesus did not suggest that we tell everyone about Jesus, He commanded us to "Go." That is an action word, so we should all get busy sharing the good news. We should handle the Word of God with great care and be doers of His mighty Word. I am reminding everyone today that we do not possess a hidden gospel. This is not a secret society but a family that everyone can belong to.

The Bible tells us, "But if our gospel be hid, it is hid to them that are lost: In whom the god of this world hath blinded the minds of them which believe not, lest the light of the glorious gospel of Christ, who is the image of God, should shine unto them" (2 Corinthians 4:3-4). Just think about that for a minute. If we hide the truth, it is hidden to them that are lost, therefore they shall remain lost. How bad must someone hate someone else that they would not share the only news that can give them life everlasting. By not sharing the gospel of Jesus, we are telling the world we do not want them to have salvation. We might as well tell them to go to hell. Brothers and sisters, this is not why we have been saved. We have been saved by the grace of God, so that we can be a blessing to others and share the same good news with others. We have been saved so that we can help save others, not to keep the truth from them so they can face eternal damnation. So let us go out this day and for the rest of our lives and share the Gospel of Jesus Christ. We should be uncovering the truth and revealing to the world the only way to salvation.

- **Read 2 Corinthians 4:1-6**
- Does knowing that you have the light of God in your heart change how you live?
- Do you remember the song, "this little light of mine"?
  o We have this light, so that we can shine and share it with others.
- Is it easy for you to share the Gospel of Jesus and your personal faith with others?
- Remember the great commission of Jesus Christ in **Mark 16:15** is a commandment, not a request.
- Take time this week to share the gospel with others you come in contact with.
- Remember, our job Is not to save anyone. Our job is to simply share the Truth in love.
- Record in a journal or diary how you shared the Gospel and with whom you shared it with.
- What were the results of that interaction?
- Regardless of the outcome, be encouraged knowing that you are doing the will of God, for his honor, glory and praise.

THE ISSUE WITH AUTHORITY

Today there are many people, young and old alike, that have a problem with authority. We can hear and see it every day. There are disgruntled workers everywhere and it spews over into the consumer's environment, which should never happen. This problem that many have with authority is ruining their lives and negatively affecting the lives of others around them because of the attitude they display. This is an actual disorder called, "Oppositional Defiant Disorder" or ODD (Brain Balance, n.d.). People with ODD are angry and are always in an irritable mood. They typically want to argue and act in a vindictive way towards authority, although not necessarily aggressively. But whether aggressive or not, nobody wants to be around a person who is always upset and always argumentative and vindictive. People who live with this disorder can change and make a positive impact on those around them.

And then there are others that do not have a disorder, they just do not like authority. I have been around many of these people. Especially when I was in the military. These people would not lash out at the authority, but they would be defiant by not following the direction given to them. Which in turn causes someone else to have to compensate for them not doing their work. When someone rebels against authority by not doing their job, that work falls on someone else. Now not only has the attitude caused a problem, but the lack of production causes a bigger issue. This is not what a Christian should display. Whether in the workplace or in our society as a whole, we are told how we should behave ourselves as children of God.

The Bible says, "Let every soul be subject unto the higher powers. For there is no power but of God: the powers that be are ordained of God" (Romans 13:1). So, if we put things into perspective, we can know that the things that go on around us have been ordained by God. Whether we see them as good or bad, things are happening because

God put things in place or allowed them to happen. Why? Perhaps you and I are supposed to be the ones that positively affect that person to change. Maybe it is your faithful prayers and actions in the workplace that causes your boss to come to know Christ. I am not suggesting that anyone suffers abuse at the hands of another person, but I am saying that not everything someone says or does is abusive. Just because we do not like the action doesn't mean it is abuse. My concern is and will always be that I conduct myself in a manner that is in line with the principles of godliness and Christianity. All I can do is control my actions and words. I cannot control those around me. Just remember that everyone is going to give an account (see Hebrews 13:17). That means you and me, your boss, co-workers, friends, family, and everybody else. Be the person God has called you to be in all you do and in every place you go. You can be the spark that starts the fire of revival in the very place you are right now.

- **Read Romans Chapter 13:1-7 & 2 Peter 13-25**
- How does knowing what God's Word says regarding authority change your opinion about how you operate, whether at home, at work, or in your everyday life?
- As we consider what often times seems as suffering under certain authorities in our lives, let us never forget that Christ also suffered.
    o Our Lord and Savior suffered far worse than anything we have faced.
- Mediate on these scriptures, knowing it is the Truth of the divinely inspired, inerrant, infallible and sufficient Word of God.
- Remember, when we rebel against those appointed over us, we are not just rebelling against them, we are going against the Word of God.
- Focus this week on submitting to God in all things and displaying a servant attitude wherever you may be.
- Pray for God to help you live according to His Word.
- Journal your thoughts and also any changes you notice around you at work, at home or in life in general based on your effort to surrendering to God's Word.

THE WORD IS NOT PROGRESSIVE

Progressive Christianity has become a hot topic in the world as of late. Many people are leaving traditional churches and have joined the progressive movement because they feel as though the church should be inclusionary and have acceptance for anyone into the Body of Christ regardless of their lifestyle. They have abandoned the Bible as the infallible, inerrant, divinely inspired Word of God as the truth, and only use the Bible as a guide. So called Pastors of these churches expand upon stories written in the Bible and manipulate them so as to condone their progressive ideals and even go as far as to indicate that you can be a Christian and still live a life of sin. This ideology has even crept into traditional Christian churches. It was recently reported that the United Methodist Church was splitting over their stance on the LGBTQ movement. One side will allow gay marriage and clergy, while the traditional church will not. Of course, this division is not limited to only the Methodists. The Southern Baptists Convention recently appointed David Uth, a pro-LGBTQ pastor as its president. The motivation seems to be that the church needs to evolve with the times.

Let me be absolutely clear; God does not change, nor does His Holy Word. I do not care what sin it is, God does not like it, and does not condone it. Yes, Jesus died for the World so that all can be saved and have eternal life (see John 3:16). But though you come to the Lord as you are, you are changed by the Holy Spirit. You are no longer your own but have been bought with a price (see 1 Corinthians 6:20 and 7:23). Therefore, we as believers in Christ live for Him and not for ourselves or for the desires of the flesh. The Bible says, "I beseech you therefore, brethren, by the mercies of God, that ye present your bodies a living sacrifice, holy, acceptable unto God, which is your reasonable service" (Romans 12:1). How can you present your bodies a living sacrifice unto

God, if you are still living in the same sin that He saved you from? The answer is simple; you cannot! Do not be fooled by these liars and false prophets that tell you it is ok to live any lifestyle you want and be saved. They are not interested in your well-being; they are only interested in filling the seats of their church. They want you to feel good so that you will come back, so they tell you what you want to hear. And in doing so they are leading the masses straight to hell.

The Bible says, "Jesus Christ the same yesterday, and to day, and for ever" (Hebrews 13:8). It also says that Jesus Christ is The Word (See John 1:1-2). And the Word says that sin is sin, and we should repent from it. Jesus says, "I tell you, Nay: but, except ye repent, ye shall all likewise perish" (Luke 13:3). Listen closely to that! Jesus says unless you repent (turn from) your sin, you shall perish (die). That is the truth! No man on the face of the earth can tell you that you will go to heaven if you continue in the sinful lifestyle. Furthermore, no man on earth can grant you passage into heaven in the first place. Only Jesus can do that. Jesus says, "I am the way, the truth, and the life. No man cometh to the Father but by me" (John 14:6). This is just another reason it is so important to read the Bible for yourselves and not to be misled by false teachers that tickle your ears with false words. It does not matter who you are or what you are doing now; Jesus will save you! He died for you. He loves you! But He wants you to come to Him with a repenting heart and be changed by His Holy Spirit. He saves us, so we can live for Him! The Word is not progressive friends. It will always remain the same and it will remain the same forever. The only thing that needs to change is us.

- **Read 1 Corinthains 6:12-20**
- How does realizing that you were bought with the precious blood of our Lord and Savior, Jesus Christ change your outlook on what you do each day?
    - How do you talk?
    - How do you eat and drink?
    - Where do you go and who do you associate with?
- Are these things pleasing unto God, or do they merely satisfy your fleshly desires?

- Focus each day this week on making a concerted effort to flee the things that are sinful and live a righteous life for the Lord's sake, the One who died to make us free.
- Pray for God to provide you with the strength to live righteously and make the changes that are needed in your life. Remember, He is the One doing the work from within.
- Don't be discouraged when you stumble, get back up, ask for forgiveness and start again. He is with you!
- Journal your experiences, both your success and your shortcomings, asking the lord to help you each day.

THE STONE THE BUILDERS REJECTED

It is amazing to me when I think about God's plan for us. His plan existed before He ever laid the foundations of the earth. Our heavenly Father knew that we would sin and provided a way for us to be reconciled to Him. He planned to send Jesus to save us from our sins before Adam & Eve ate of the tree of the knowledge of good and evil. God's Word is true and provides so much wisdom and insight for us, if we would only read it, study it, live it, and share it. One thing that stands out to me in the Holy Bible is that God provided Himself as the perfect sacrifice so that all who believe can have eternal life with Him, basking in His glory. God sent Jesus Christ, His only begotten son (read John 3:16) to die in our place.

The same Messiah that was prophesied hundreds of years beforehand, was and is indeed the Word of God who became flesh and dwelt among us (See John 1:1-2). But I believe some people have not given much thought as to why you and I, who are not Jews, were able to receive this precious gift of salvation. People forget that Jesus came to save the Jews. The Jews had been anticipating the Messiah to come and save them for centuries. But when He came and walked among them, they rejected Him. They accused Him falsely, beat Him brutally, humiliated Him publicly, and murdered Him unjustly on the cross at calvary.

As brutal and heinous these things are that they did to our Lord, it was all part of God's plan. Jesus came into this world willingly and knowing exactly what He was going to do. He did it knowing that the people that God called the "apple of His eye" (Lamentations 2:18, Zechariah 2:8, et.al.) would reject Him. Yet this very man, the Messiah that was prophesied of, the Son of God that was rejected by the Jews, is the head of the Church. The Bible says, "Jesus saith unto them, Did ye never read in the scriptures, The stone which the builders rejected, the same is become the head of the corner: this is the Lord's doing, and it is marvellous in our eyes?" (Matthew 21:42). Indeed, the stone that the Jews rejected is our chief corner stone. He came to save the Jews, but He also knew they would reject Him and turned His attention to the World because of it. And He had this planed before Adam and Eve ever sinned against Him.

Although Jesus is the Messiah that the Hebrew prophets foretold would come and save them, He is also the savior of the world for all who call upon Him and believe in Him. The Word of Truth says, "For God so loved the world, that he gave his only begotten Son, that whosoever believeth in him should not perish, but have everlasting life" (John 3:16). It also says, "For whosoever shall call upon the name of the Lord shall be saved" (Romans 10:13). Oh, what a Savior! If you have not called upon His name, I urge you to do so today. Do not reject the chief corner stone. If you have accepted Jesus as your personal Savior, tell someone else about Him so they can share in the joy and glory of the Lord.

- **Read John 3:16**
- Have you placed your trust and faith in Jesus for Salvation?
- If not, what is keeping you from doing so?
- If you have, are you freely sharing Jesus with the world around you so that they might be saved as well?
- **Read Romans 10:9-10 & 13.**
- Even though Jesus came to save the lost sheep of Isarel, His plan always included the world.
- Knowing that Christ died for the world, and not just a select few, How does this affect how you present Him to others?
  - o Do you want to keep Him all to yourself?
- Focus this week on sharing the Gospel message of the death, burial and resurrection of our Lord and Savior Jesus Christ with others.
- Tell them the good news and share how a relationship with Jesus has changed your life with them as well.
- Pray for the courage to share Christ with others.
- Journal your experience this week, remembering that not everyone will receive it.
  - o Again, our job is to be obedient, not to save a soul.

RUNNING THE RACE

When I was a young man, I use to run road races. The longest one I ran was only a 10K, or 6.2 miles, but most were simple 5k (3.1 mile) races. I was so used to running back then that sometimes after registering for the race I would let my training slide because I knew that with very little effort, I could complete the race. Instead of training I wanted to do other things that all of my friends were doing. Rather than get up in the morning and go for a jog, I would sleep in because I had a late night with my friends. However, when I started running in the event, I soon noticed many people passing me as I labored to breathe, and my legs grew heavier, and my body tired quickly. Sometimes I even had to walk to finish the race looking as though I was a cardiac victim rather than a participant in a run. I was not properly prepared to run these specific events and it showed. I had no endurance, and it was evident in my performance. This reminds me of scripture in the Bible about our relationship and walk with Christ.

Hebrews 12:1-2 says, "Wherefore seeing we also are compassed about with so great a cloud of witnesses, let us lay aside every weight, and the sin which doth so easily beset us, and let us run with patience the race that is set before us, looking unto Jesus the author and finisher of our faith; who for the joy that was set before him endured the cross, despising the shame, and is set down at the right hand of the throne of God". The word "beset" means to trouble or threaten persistently. Today many Christians start out quickly, on fire for the Lord. Yet soon after they fade into the darkness of the crowd that surrounds them and give up the race entirely. They lack endurance to complete the race set before them. Why? Because they are not properly trained. They may pray but fail to read their Bible to allow Jesus to speak to them. One-way communication is not communication at all; you must have feedback in order to have a good talk. After all, we are supposed to be looking unto Jesus, the author and finisher of our faith. How can this be if we never look to His Word and listen to Him speak?

Even though we live in a world surrounded by non-believers on every side that tell us it is ok to live for self; Jesus tells us differently. While we may be mocked for our beliefs, we must continue in the life that is now ours. Jesus endured more suffering than you or I could ever imagine. Remember, we have not yet suffered unto death or shed our blood for our faith. Jesus on the other hand did and He did so for us, so that we may be free from the bondage of sin. The scripture says for the joy that was set before Him he did this for us. We should look unto Jesus continually as our example to follow as we run the race set before us. We should also be laser focused on the Joy to come and not on the circumstances we currently live in. Although we may have the burden of a sinful world around us, let us lay that down and run this race with patience and endurance.

- **Read Hebrews 12:1-4 & 1 Corinthians 9:24-27**
- How does knowing we have a "cloud of witnesses" surrounding us, change how you view your walk with Christ?
- Does it make you more anxious about your faith, or does it give you greater strength and encouragement? I pray it is the latter.
- Knowing that Christ is the author and finisher of our faith, take some time in meditation and prayer to thank God for His free gift of salvation, and ask Him to continue to sustain you in your walk with Jesus.
- Ask God to light your path, establish your steps and keep you running the race that He has set before you to run. For your good, and for His Glory.
- Remembering the pain and affliction that Jesus endured before and during His crucifixion, I encourage you to endure with your head held high, looking toward the finish line.
- Be encouraged! We will all celebrate victoriously in Heaven, gathered around the Throne of Glory!
   o With an incorruptible crown!

- Spend time in prayer this week asking God for the strength and endurance to continue this race of the life we live, looking for the glorious life to come.
- Journal your thoughts and experiences this week as you focus on continuing to live for Christ in obedience and sharing the Gospel.

MEEKNESS IS NOT A WEAKNESS

In Matthew 5:5 Jesus says, "Blessed are the meek: for they shall inherit the earth." In today's culture one assumes that anyone who is meek must be weak. The reason is simple. The term meek today is defined as "deficient in spirit or courage" and "not violent or strong" according to Merriam-Webster. People commonly use the term meek to describe someone who is powerless or submissive due to necessity. In other words, we think of someone being meek because that particular person cannot defend themselves. However, in the days of Jesus, this term was not used to describe someone who was weak or deficient in spirit or courage. On the contrary, it was used to describe the strongest of all. Jesus Himself is an example of a meek person and He is the absolute example that we as Christians should strive to be like.

In the days, that Jesus walked the earth in the flesh, the term meek actually meant to describe have the "power to absorb adversity and criticism without lashing back." (Piper, 1986). If you think about this for a minute you will understand why Jesus was described as meek. He had the power to call down ten thousand angels to save him from the judgement of man and the death of the cross. Yet even though He could have used His power He chose to submit Himself to the Father's plan for our salvation. He gave Himself up freely and died on the cross at Calvary so that whosoever calls upon His name could live forever. That is the most powerful example of meekness that anyone could ever show.

Another way to think of meekness is to think of the word "tame" as it is used to describe animals. A tame lion has the power to destroy and conquer just as it was created to survive and dominate in the wild. However, because it is "tame" the lion becomes submissive to the situation and environment in which it now lives. You and I have power as humans. Some of us have undergone physical training that gives us more power over others in regard to physical stature and knowledge. For example, someone who has become a Navy Seal would have a lot more knowledge and skill than the average citizen on the street. However, the Seal now understands the power they were given but does not use it just to have dominion over the average Joe on the street. By their virtues, they have become meek.

This is what Jesus is referring to in Matthew 5:5. Individually, you and I may have the power and skill to overcome others and take advantage of the situation to our benefit on earth. But Jesus tells us to be meek. Jesus wants us to control our emotions and become more like Him. That does not mean we get railroaded or totally give up the right to defend ourselves against legitimate threats, but it does mean to submit to His authority over our lives. How? By going to God in prayer and reading our Bibles daily so that He can instruct us on what to do and how to behave. We as Christians must submit ourselves to His authority and quit relying on our own strength, power, and knowhow to manage situations. We should let go and let God. Just remember the words of Jesus… "Blessed are the meek, for they shall inherit the earth."

- **Read Matthew 5, Psalm 37 focusing on verses 9,11, & 22**
- Have you ever considered meekness a superpower?
- Even though many today think of someone who is meek and mild mannered as being weak, we know that meekness was displayed by the most powerful of all, our Lord Jesus Christ.
- How does the definition of "restrained strength" for meekness change your outlook on being or becoming meek?
- We should strive everyday to be more Christ like, and since He displayed meekness, we should strive to display meekness in our lives each day as well.
- This week, focus on displaying a meeker attitude even in the face of those around you acting hostile.
- Remember as part of the beatitudes, Jesus says the meek will inherit the earth.
- Remember, the Lord sees those who are trying to tempt you and negatively affect you. He will handle those people as well.

- Pray for those who are trying your patients and ask God for strength to overcome and grant you the superpower of meekness.
- Journal your thoughts regarding this topic and record how your interactions have changed based implementing the teachings of Jesus in your life.

FEAR FACTOR

There used to be a show on television called Fear Factor where contestants would face their fears for the chance to win money. Contestants would have to answer a questionnaire before they were selected regarding their biggest fears and then usually had to face those same fears when they were on the show. Yet these same people could overcome their fear for just a chance at a reward. And today I see people that are afraid to go to the grocery store because they fear they may contract the virus that the Journal of American Medical Association says has only a 2.3% fatality rate. The actual numbers associated with this latest pandemic show that nearly 81% of people that contracted the virus have "mild" symptoms, and less deadly than SARS (Sandoiu, 2020). Yet people are acting like this is the Black Plague.

As a Christian I can honestly say that we need not be afraid of anything. I know this flies in the face of reason and will also likely upset many Christians who may have placed themselves in a self-quarantine. However, I would like to help alleviate some of the fear that many are living with today from a biblical perspective. Even though we should be smart and do our part in helping to not spread the virus, especially to those with weakened immune systems, we should not live in fear. God created us to be fearless in His righteousness and to stand on the promises in His Word. The Bible says, "The oath which he sware to our father Abraham, That he would grant unto us, that we being delivered out of the hand of our enemies might serve him without fear, In holiness and righteousness before him, all the days of our life" (Luke 1:73-75). The emphasis here is on serving our Lord without fear all the days of our lives. Fear is of the devil and the devil is our chief enemy.

I understand the natural reaction is to be fearful because we still live in a fleshly body and often times our flesh likes to overrule in things that matter. However, we as Christians need to die to self and rely on the Holy Spirit who lives in each of us. I live in fear today, but it is the fear of the Lord. It is a righteous and reverent fear for God Almighty and doing what He has instructed me to do through His Holy Word is the most important thing to me. It should also be the most important thing to all Christians, even to the point of overcoming the natural fear of the flesh. Peter says, "And if ye call on the Father, who without respect of persons judgeth according to every man's work, pass the time of your sojourning here in fear:" (1 Peter 1:17). I pass the time God has allotted me on earth in reverent fear of the Most High, not the fear of the world or what it has to offer, including a virus.

Yes, we should all take precautions so as to not be negligent and help prevent the spread of the virus to those who have compromised immune systems, because those are the ones the virus can harm the most. But do not be afraid to go to the grocery store, to walk down the street, or to assemble in church. John reminds us, "Ye are of God, little children, and have overcome them: because greater is he that is in you, than he that is in the world" (1 John 1:4). We are overcomers because He who lives in us has overcome the world. Live without fear knowing that God is in control and has ordained all things. We do not have to understand the why of the matter, we just have to understand Who is in complete control.

Christians know where we are going when we pass from this world, so we should not live in fear of what this world has to offer. It is a win-win situation. If we live then we get to live for Christ and continue to spread the good news of the Gospel, which is what He created us to do. The alternative for Christians is to be with Him forever. Paul says, "We are confident, I say, and willing rather to be absent from the body, and to be present with the Lord" (2 Corinthians 5:8). So, let me encourage you in this current season brothers and sisters; be smart, but do not fear… "For the Lord, thy God is with you withersoever thou goest" (Joshua 1:9b).

- **Read Joshua 1:9, Psalm 27:1-2, Luke 12:4-7 & 2 Timothy 1:7**
- Understanding what God has commanded us regarding fear, do you find yourself still living fearful?

- I pray that you be strong in the faith and courageous, especially in times of doubt, trial and tribulation. Lean on God and His Holy Word and do not rely on your own understanding.
- Pray for God to grant you this courage and power to overcome the fear. The Holy Spirit of God is in you, and He will lead you.
- As you encounter fearful situations in your life from this point forward, recite Joshua 1:9 and 2 Timothy 1:7. Let them be a reminder of who you are in Christ and that you have God inside you.
- Exercise your courage through your faith in Christ.
- Journal your experiences and write down specific incidents in your life where you have been fearful, and when you were able to overcome those fears.
- Speak with other Christians about being strong and courageous in Christ Jesus and walk together in times of turmoil. Partners in Christ are extremely beneficial.

GOD'S JUDGEMENT

In reading the Old Testament you will find several times throughout the history of the Jewish people where they turned from following God and His commandments and began living according to the lust of the flesh and seeking after the ways of foreign people. God clearly told His people not to intermingle their faith and by virtue of seeking deals with other nations that is exactly what happened. The Jewish people quit living according to the ways of God. However, God, who had brought them out of captivity, and established them as a nation in a land of milk and honey continued to try to get their attention over and over again.

As I examine Jeremiah chapter 5, I cannot help but see the similarities between the Jewish people of that day and Christians today. God says through the prophet in verse two, "And they say, The Lord liveth; surely they swear falsely." Just like in the ancient days of Israel we have many today that proclaim the name of Jesus but do so for their own vain glory and not for the glory, honor and praise of the Lord Jesus Christ. There are numerous people shouting "Lord, Lord" who have no true idea who the Lord is. How do we know these people? We know them by their fruit. We know them by their actions. If their actions do not line up with their words, and more importantly with the words of the Bible, then they swear falsely.

The interesting thing to note from studying the Old Testament is that God did not let this type of behavior go unpunished. He loves His people and wants the best for them and leads them according to His will, but when men stray from the path of righteousness, He tries to correct their paths gently. When the gentle nudging does not work, God increases his methods until He gets their full and undivided attention. Just like in the time of Jeremiah I believe God is trying to get humanity's attention today before it is too late. Before the ultimate judgement that is to come, God is using other means to bring people to repentance. The Lord's eyes are on the truth and knows the heart of man. God cannot be fooled by the deceitfulness of man. God continues in Jeremiah by saying, "How shall I pardon thee for this? thy children have forsaken me and sworn by them that are no gods: when I had fed them to the full, they then committed adultery, and assembled themselves by troops in the harlots' houses" (Jeremiah 5:7).

Just like in the times past, God is telling us today to remember Him; to return to the one who has provided our every need and has blessed us. As Christians in America, we do not need to look too far in the past to see how we once were. When you compare our young history as a nation, formed on the principles of the Bible and as believers in Jesus Christ, to our current situation as a nation some two hundred forty-eight years later, there should be no doubt as to why we face the trials we do today. We have forsaken God and have committed adultery and assembled our troops in the harlot's house. We have intermingled our faith with the faith of strangers and strange gods who are no gods at all.

What is worse is that some so-called pastors, preachers, and evangelists have gone the same deceitful way. They preach for their own vain glory knowing the more they tickle the ears the more they will be celebrated by a people that have gone astray. They know as long as they tell people what they want to hear, the people will come back. They speak to fill seats not to fill hearts with truth. God said, "The prophets prophesy falsely, and the priests bear rule by their means; and my people love to have it so: and what will ye do in the end thereof" (Jeremiah 5:31)?

Let me be the first to tell you, this shall not go without its reward. However, we are getting ever so closer to the day in which Jesus will call his bride home and the church will be no more on earth. The judgement to come is not one from which you can recover. The final judgement will not end well for those who have refused to believe in the Jesus Christ, and for all those who falsely claimed to represent Him. I pray today that people will turn from the evil of the world, the deceitfulness of false prophets, and put their full trust in the Lord Jesus Christ.

Read Jeremiah Chapter 5 (I Recommend reading the entire book)

- As you gather information about the history of God's chosen people (Israel) do you see the parallels with modern Christians today?
- Do you think people have a complete understanding of who God is and what he desires from us?
- As you draw closer to Christ by studying His Word and praying daily, take time to pray for the Churches in your community.
    - Pray for their pastors and the congregations, that they will seek after the Truth and live according to it.
    - Pray for those specifically that you know are lost and, on the outside, looking in, that they will receive the Gospel of Jesus Christ and place their faith and trust in Him for salvation.
- In your journal, record some observations within the community and within your circles without naming names.
    - Are there definitive issues that are in direct opposition of the Word of God?
    - Pray for those people and/or the circumstances surrounding them.
- Ask God to help you live a Godlier life and to be an example for others to follow.

HE IS RISEN

A week before Jesus' death on the Cross at Calvary, He was welcomed into Jerusalem riding on a colt while the people gathered to see His triumphant entry waved palm branches. Zechariah prophesied of this very occasion in Zechariah 9:9 around five hundred years before Jesus' time. Yet, a week after His jubilant entry, the one who came to save us from our sins would die on a lowly cross on the Hill of Golgotha called Calvary. God told us through His Word that He would send the Messiah, but few believed that Jesus was Him. If you examine the story of Abraham and Isaac all the way back in Genesis some 1900 years before Christ lived amongst us, you will see a picture of God's saving grace even then. God told Abraham to take His son Isaac to a place where He would show him and instructed Abraham to offer his son for a sacrifice.

Abraham did as he was instructed, but Isaac looked around and noticed they had everything for a sacrifice but a lamb. Isaac asked his father, "Behold the fire and the wood: but where is the lamb for a burnt offering?" (Genesis 22:7b). But Abraham answered in a faithful manner, knowing that God had promised to make Abraham's seed a great nation. "And Abraham said, my son, God will provide himself a lamb for a burnt offering: so they went both of them together" (Genesis 22:8). Isaac was not sacrificed that day because God provided a substitute for Isaac, just as He has provided a substitute for you and me. Mt. Moriah was where Abraham took Isaac that faithful day. Mt. Moriah would later become the place of the Temple Mount in Jerusalem. The Temple Mount and Calvary share the same limestone ridgeline. The same place where God provided a substitute for Isaac, He provided a substitute for us.

Within a week of, Jesus was betrayed by Judas, tried by the Jews and brought before Pontius Pilate and sentenced to death. Jesus, the only one who was perfect and innocent of sin, was sentenced to death for our sake. The perfect lamb, without blemish that Abraham prophesied about was here to lay down His life as the perfect substitute for the sin of man. God indeed did provide Himself a sacrifice for man. Jesus, God incarnate, the lamb without blemish, the only one guiltless of sin, took our sin and bare it on the cross. He laid down His life so that we could live forever with Him in Glory. All we have to do is believe in our hearts and confess that Jesus is Lord. And after He died, they took His body and placed it in the tomb of a man named Joseph of Arimathea and sealed the tomb with a stone and bound the stone so that no one would tamper with the grave.

The Romans even placed guards in front of the stone as to keep people from trying to take the Body of Christ away. The disciples of Jesus were crushed and the people who followed Jesus and His teachings were in disbelief. How could the Messiah, the one who came to save us, be dead? But just as Jesus Himself prophesied, he did not stay in the grave. As Jesus had spoken before, "…Destroy this temple, and in three days I will raise it up" (John 2:19), after three days that His body laid in the grave He resurrected. The grave could not hold Him!

Scripture records that when the two Mary's went to the sepulcher on the first of the week, there was a great earthquake, and the Angel of the lord rolled the stone away from the grave and sat upon the stone. "And the angel answered and said unto the women, Fear not ye: for I know that ye seek Jesus, which was crucified. He is not here: for he is risen, as he said. Come, see the place where the Lord lay" (Matthew 28:5-6). We who are covered by the blood of Jesus Christ need not worry. We share in a promise from God that where He is, we shall also be. Because He rose again, we know our bodies shall rise again too. I pray that your faith be emboldened today and rejoice in the Lord and know that He is Risen!

Read All of Genesis 22 (focus on verses 7-8) John 2:19 & Matthew 28:1-10

- Can you see the glorious plan of God from the beginning?
- God knew Adam and Eve would disobey and he had a plan of redemption from even before the foundation of the World was laid.

- We have a saying that the Old Testament is the New Testament Concealed and the New Testament is the Old Testament revealed.
  - o I pray that you can se that comparing the story of Abraham and Isaac with the Death, Burial and Resurrection of Christ.
- God loves His creation and all He wants is our relationship restored.
  - o He provided the only way. The Lamb of God, who taketh away the sins of the world!
  - o All we have to do is confess and believe in our heart.
- This week spend some time alone with God n prayer just praising Him and thanking Him for restoring you to fellowship with Him through the precious blood of His only begotten son, Jesus Christ.
- Invite an unbeliever to Christ by giving them the Gospel and invite them to Church.
  - o Pray for them and with them.
- Record in your journal how the story of redemption that saved your soul has impacted your life!

YE SHALL RECEIVE POWER

Most people that are not saved do not understand everything that transpires for a newly saved Christian. Some think that it is merely traditional symbolism when someone accepts Christ. They believe that person simply has followed his or her friends and family through ritualistic church proceedings. And while there may be some who profess Christianity who have simply mouthed words without belief in their heart, I can assure you that there is a miraculous life transforming event that occurs for the born-again believer in Christ Jesus. In fact, there is an immediate response from God to the prayerful soul of a sinner who calls upon the name of Jesus. Jesus himself told the apostles about it before he was crucified.

While Jesus lived, the apostles saw many marvelous works that he performed; He turned water into wine, walked on water, healed the sick, caused the lame to walk, gave sight back to the blind, and even raised the dead in the presence of numerous people. Even prior to Jesus' birth, God worked many miracles from the beginning of creation via the angel of the Lord in certain instances. He also delivered his people by speaking to and acting through prophets and patriarchs such as Abraham, Isaac, Jacob, Joseph, Noah, Moses, Samuel, and David just to name a few. But these people were given certain gifts and words from God while others that were alive at the time were without. An everyday citizen of the world did not possess any special ability to accomplish anything extraordinary unless God presented those to them in specific situations. But today is different. God has given anyone who calls upon the name of Jesus power!

Jesus told his apostles," But ye shall receive power, after that the Holy Ghost is come upon you: and ye shall be witnesses unto me both in Jerusalem, and in all Judaea, and in Samaria, and unto the uttermost part of the earth" (Acts 1:8). You see, prior to Jesus' death burial and resurrection, people did not possess the Holy Spirit. In order for the apostles to receive the Holy Comforter, Jesus had to lay down his life, be resurrected and ascend into heaven again. But He told them they would receive power once the Holy Ghost came upon them. On the day of Pentecost fifty days after the Crucifixion, that is exactly what happened. The Apostles received the power of the Holy Spirit and began to speak in the tongues (languages) of other people. This was done so that those that spoke other languages gathered nearby could understand the words and also believe. Those people were astonished that these common and uneducated men were speaking in their languages. The Holy Spirit had entered into the Apostles on this day.

Jesus has given us His Word, "Verily, verily, I say unto you, He that believeth on me, the works that I do shall he do also; and greater works than these shall he do; because I go unto my Father" (John 14:12). How can we do greater works than those that we read about? Because we believe on the name of Jesus. The moment a sinner confesses Christ, asks for forgiveness of sins, repents, and accepts Jesus Christ as Lord and Savior, the Holy Spirit enters into the body and resides forever. You cannot lose Him. He will not forsake you or leave you! A Christian possesses the power of God by the Holy Spirit living inside them through faith in Jesus. Today I encourage every Christian to pray and put the power of the Holy Spirit to work in the world. Pray for those outside the body of Christ to come to know Jesus as Lord and Savior. Pray for God's will to be done. Pray for God's Kingdome to come. If you want to see the power of God at work through you, pray for God's will and believe and it shall be done.

Read Acts Chapter 1:1-5 & 2:1-13.

- Do you know you have the Power of the Holy Spirit living inside you?
    - o That means you have power!
    - o But we have previously studied that we do not do things or seek things for our own vain glory, or our own desires. We seek to do the Father's Will and that is how we pray.

- The same power that saves you from eternal condemnation is the same power that will keep you from living in sin.
  - In other words, the power that saved you from the punishment of sin, is the same that keeps us from sinning.
  - We can adhere to the Holy Spirit, or we can ignore Him and grieve Him.
    - If you have fallen prey to sin after salvation, might I point you to **1 John 1:9**.
- We should be seeking to do the Lord's Will.
  - If we seek to do so, He will equip us and give us the authority and power to execute it.
  - We just need to be obedient to Him.
- How does knowing you have the Power of God within you, change how you live your life?
- I encourage you to live confidently, knowing He can and will use you to execute His Will, if you allow Him to work for His glory, honor and praise, and not your own fleshly desires.
- Pray and thank God for saving you and for living in you, and through you!

THE REBUKE OF THE WISE

Have you ever been mad at someone you love and trust because they said something to you that crushed your spirit? Perhaps they were trying to help you by correcting you or giving you a piece of advice for whatever you were going through at that moment. Human beings are certainly fickle creatures. On one hand we want people to love us, and on the other hand we only want love to come in a way that always makes us feel good. But the truth is love sometimes hurts. Telling someone something they need to hear, albeit hard, is a form of love when that information could ultimately help someone else. Surrounding ourselves with people who always tell us what we want to hear can lead to our own demise. Misery loves company as they say.

The Bible says, "It is better to hear the rebuke of the wise, than for a man to hear the song of fools" (Ecclesiastes 7:5). King Solomon tells us that we should desire to have those around us that love us enough to tell us the truth in all circumstances. Even when that truth is not as popular as the lie that people are living around us. Yet many today surround themselves with fools who continue to spread their foolish misery to others. People are often comforted by others in the same situation as they are and hang on their every word not realizing that the advice they are receiving is terribly bad advice altogether. If I were drowning, I would not ask someone else who was drowning for help. I would look for someone with a life preserver. But people today that find themselves in bad situations look for others in the same tough situation and seek their opinions on how to improve their state of affairs. What is more is that people will absolutely lose their minds when a loved one attempts to help them by giving them sound advice.

Telling a drug addict or alcoholic that they need help is not received well by most addicts. I have known some and have even offered to help them only to be rebuked by the addict and slandered in the process.

Why? The answer is pride. Those people feel as though you are judging them, and they really do not want to give up the very thing that is causing their misery. They would rather wallow in filth and complain about being dirty than to be washed and made clean once and for all. Once someone has sunk so low into a dark world it is hard to help them because they are singing the songs of fools. But it is not impossible to help them. The Bible tells us, "…The things which are impossible with men are possible with God" (Luke 18:27). So, it is imperative that we do not give up trying to help those in need. And when they refuse sound advice and rebuke you for being judgmental, continue to pray for them. Even if they never want to see you or speak to you again, continue to pray for them. God can change them. God can take the broken and make them whole. And more than anything, no matter what, do not let the song of the fools deter you from being of a sober mind and doing what Jesus has asked the faithful to do. One day the foolish may become wise in the same manner that we all did: by the grace of God.

Read Ecclesiastes 7:5 Psalm 141:5, Proverbs 9:8, 15:31–32, 17:10, 27:6.

- Have you ever given advice that was not well received?
    - o Was it sound Godly advice as from a friend?
- Have you ever been given advice that you did not receive well from a Godly friend?
    - o How did you receive it?
    - o I have told my adult kids before, that even if it comes from someone that doesn't like you or that is unfriendly, if the information is truthful, receive it with grace.
    - o Sometimes we have to swallow our own pride and receive advice or constructive criticism from those we would rather not.
        - ▪ The truth is the truth, no matter whose mouth it came from.
- I pray that we all as Christians can accept criticism when it presented and examine ourselves in accordance with it.

- o Good godly advice from Christian friends is essential to growing in our relationship with the Lord as well.
  - o Proverbs_27:17 says, "Iron sharpeneth iron; so a man sharpeneth the countenance of his friend."
- This week, let us concentrate on being that friend who not only can give good Godly counsel, but can also receive it from others in a Christlike manner.
- Thank God in prayer for Godly friends and Godly counselors.
- Journal your encounters that you have when giving and receiving counsel.

WHO'S CONDEMNING WHO?

A lot of people living in the world today and who are not saved, think that Christians are judgmental people who are only condemning everyone who is not saved and going to church. They feel as though the eyes of the church are upon them in a negative way and some even suggest that this is the reason they do not come to church and commit their lives to Jesus. While I understand their argument, the argument is flawed from the get-go. I have been the person on the "outside looking in"; the one who felt like he was being judged by everyone in the church because of the way I dressed and talked, because of the tattoos that I got earlier in my life, and because of the job I may have held at a particular point in my life. But once I understood who was placing those thoughts in my head, I realized it was not the world that was judging me, but the devil himself. After all, it is Satan who is our enemy, not our brothers and sisters, neighbors, or any other flesh and blood person.

The Bible tells us "For we wrestle not against flesh and blood, but against principalities, against powers, against rulers of the darkness of this world, against spiritual wickedness in high places" (Ephesians 6:12). The devil likes to use our own emotions against us and try to get us to believe that our enemy are the ones God has saved. He is very subtle and will use every tactic in the world for his benefit. His plan is to deter you from knowing the truth, being saved, and living a life that glorifies God.

Many people know or at least have heard of John 3:16; "For God so loved the World that He gave His only begotten Son, that whosoever believeth in Him shall not perish, but have everlasting life." It is the very first verse I ever learned as a kid, and for many years it was just a routine scripture I quoted without giving thought to the significant impact that the verse has on humanity. I now know that this verse, and the entire Bible, is God explaining to humanity that we do not have to die for our sins. We do not have to face eternal condemnation. Just one verse later Jesus explains this when He says, "For God sent not his Son into the world to condemn the world; but that the world through him might be saved" (John 3:17).

Jesus came so that we do not have to be condemned. All we have to do is accept Jesus Christ as the Son of God, who is God incarnate, and believe in His finished works of the death, burial and resurrection, and we are saved. The bible tells us, "For whosoever shall call upon the name of the Lord shall be saved" (Romans 10:13). But the devil likes to use our emotions against us. Satan likes to twist the truth into a lie and get people to believe that the church is judgmental, and all Christians do is judge one another and look down their noses at people outside of the Body of Christ. But the real truth is it is the exact opposite. Our job as Christians is to reach the world with the gospel and to make disciples of everyone. But it has often been said that the truth hurts, and indeed it does.

The Bible says, "For the word of God is quick, and powerful, and sharper than any twoedged sword, piercing even to the dividing asunder of soul and spirit, and of the joints and marrow, and is a discerner of the thoughts and intents of the heart" (Hebrews 4:12). It most certainly pierced my heart and caused an internal battle which led to my repentance. The Word caused me to turn from the world and to the Lord. But I know the struggle that many face today. I know the wicked tactics that the serpent likes to use to get us away from God.

Unfortunately, many are falling for this trick and are dead in their sins. They are believing a lie and forsaking the truth. Satan has used their emotions and feelings of judgement to keep them from eternal salvation. If we continue to read in John chapter three, we will see that the condemnation that the Lord came to save us from is already upon those who do not believe. "He that believeth on him is not condemned: but he that believeth not is condemned already, because he hath not believed in the name of the only begotten Son of God" (John 3:18). If you believe the truth, you are saved for eternity. However, if you do not believe, you are condemned already. It isn't the Church that is judging and condemning. It is the devil, and many are still falling for his old tricks.

Read John 3:16-18, Ephesians 6:12, Hebrews 4:12, and Romans 10:9-10,13.

- Have you ever felt like you were judged by a Christian or Church goer?
- Being completely honest, have you ever judged someone else?
- People will often say they don't like being judged, but they themselves judge in the process.
  - o I was once judged by a man telling me why he wouldn't come to church; the man said something to the effect of "I can't be around all you church folk because you look down on people like me".
    - Oh, I could think was, "wow, you know an awful lot about me to have never met me".
  - o We as Christians on the other hand have to use discernment (which is Godly judgement) to keep us from being where we shouldn't be, and doing things we shouldn't be doing. Sometimes that entails not being around specific people or groups of people.
    - The Bible says to "Abstain from all appearance of evil" (1 Thessalonians 5:22), "And have no fellowship with the unfruitful works of darkness, but rather reprove them' (Ephesians 5:11).
    - Now how are we to do this without judging righteously?
- We are not judging who can be saved and who cannot be saved. We are not condemning anyone to hell. We don't have that authority. The Gospel is for everyone because Jesus died for the world.
  - o Let us therefore spread the Gospel and welcome any and all into the fold.
    - However, we need to help them grow in their walk as well.
    - That goes hand in hand with the last devotional of the rebuke of the wise.

- Pray and ask God to guide you in Godly wisdom through His Word.
  - Ask Him to give you the gift of discernment and thank Him for opening your eyes to the truth in His Word and for the free gift of salvation.
- This week focus on going out of your way and out of your comfort zone to present the Gospel and invite to Church someone who you might otherwise not have previously spoken to.
  - Remember we don't save; we are just being obedient.

THE PREPARATION

In Matthew chapter 26, verses 6 through 13 we read the story of a woman with an alabaster box of precious ointment. She uses the ointment to pour on the head of Jesus as He and the disciples were eating. However, as she was doing so the disciples became outraged. More specifically, Judas Iscariot became angered regarding what the woman was doing. As we study the harmony of the gospels, we find in Mark 14:5 and John 12:5 that it was this Judas, the betrayer, that spoke about the worth of the ointment she was pouring out on Jesus. He even says that they could have sold the ointment and received three hundred pence for it. Yet Jesus says something very prophetic in her defense. "When Jesus understood it, he said unto them, why trouble ye the woman? for she hath wrought a good work upon me. For ye have the poor always with you; but me ye have not always. For in that she hath poured this ointment on my body, she did it for my burial" (Matthew 26:10-12).

Jesus told the disciples in a few sentences, yet again, that his departure was among them. He was telling them that He was preparing to physically leave them. And this woman, who the gospel of John names as Mary, was giving unto her Lord of the absolute best she had at that moment. She was giving of her most precious belongings to the Lord of Lords and the King of Kings. She undoubtedly knew who Jesus was. She was aware of the miracles He had performed and that He was truly the promised Messiah that the Jewish prophets spoke of many years before. She was not worried about how much money she was losing in the process of serving her Lord. She was not concerned about the riches she could have, only with the riches that were in front of her.

Oh, that we Christians today would be of the same mindset. We should not be concerned with tomorrow or what we may or may not have or receive. We should be concerned with having our precious

Lord right in front of us. We should be concerned with pouring out everything we have for Him. Jesus gave His life for us, so that all who believe have everlasting life. He poured out His blood for us, what are we pouring out for Him? Are we more concerned with how much we will gain tomorrow, or are we concerned with being the salt of the earth and the light of the world for His glory, honor and praise?

We could learn a lot from this passage in the Bible. One thing that we should focus on is how the King was being prepared for His departure. Even as Mary was preparing for the Lord to leave them, we should be preparing for His return. We should be pouring out our love unto Him, and for Him in an effort to prepare for that day when He calls His church home. We should gather together, sing His praises, and worship Jesus with all we have. We should be telling others about the love, mercy and saving grace of the Lord. We should be making the bride ready for the wedding day, rather than being concerned with what we may receive here on earth today or tomorrow.

However, today I see more people concerned with their own wealth, status, and achievements than they are with doing what Christ has told us to do. "And he said unto them, Go ye into all the world, and preach the gospel to every creature: (Mark 16:15). Are we doing that? "Jesus said unto him, Thou shalt love the Lord thy God with all thy heart, and with all thy soul, and with all thy mind. This is the first and great commandment. And the second is like unto it, Thou shalt love thy neighbour as thyself" (Matthew 22:37-39). Are we doing that? Just as the day of Christ's departure was upon Mary and the disciples then, the day of the church's departure is upon us today. Rather than trouble ourselves with the things of this world, let us make ready for the Lord and prepare the way for the King.

Read Matthew 26:6-13, Mark 14:3-9, John 12:1-8, Acts 1:6-11, 1 Thessalonians 4:13-18

- Just as Mary was preparing Jesus for his death, burial and resurrection, we should be preparing for His return.
- How does knowing the Truth that Jesus is alive and will return for the Church soon, shape how you live your daily life?

- Are you telling others about the saving Grace of God through faith in Jesus?
- Are you growing in your relationship each day by studying His Word, and in prayer?
- Are you living a life in a manner where others know you are different, set apart, and Holy unto the Lord?
- When you pray, do you ask for his kingdom to come?
    - o Remember that is also part of the Lord's prayer.
    - o Are you looking forward to His return?
    - o Are you seeking His return?
- This week ask the Lord in prayer to show you ways to help prepare the way for His return by witnessing and being the light in this dark world.
- Write in your journal anything that God led you to do for His glory, honor and praise this week.

SOLOMON'S SONG

I recently re-read the Old Testament book "The Song of Solomon" trying to fully understand why God ordained that this poetic writing should be in the Bible. I have always wondered why it was included from the very first time I ever read it. It is so beautifully written in romantic prose that it should have made Elizabeth Barret Browning envious. However, there is not any mention of God anywhere in the scripture. Not one instance of His Holy name or any reference to salvation by grace or the Holy Ghost. It is just simply a love letter between King Solomon's young Shulamite wife and the King himself. And, like I already mentioned, I have often wondered why it is there. But this past week as I was studying the short book, the Holy Spirit finally revealed some significant things to me regarding this wonderful story of affection.

I once heard my late Pastor preach about returning to "our first love," meaning Jesus Christ himself. Let us face it, sometimes we Christians get busy with life and wander off and some forget to come back to Christ. People forget about the saving grace of God and the wonderful free gift of salvation made possible by the love of God through Jesus when he gave his life for all who believe. We forget that God loves us so much that He was and is willing to do whatever it takes to draw you nearer to Him so that you can have everlasting life with Him. The Song of Solomon is a wonderful picture of the adoration that two can have for each other.

It reminds me of when I was first married, and how all I ever wanted was to be around my bride. All I wanted was to see her smile, hear her laugh, and hold her hand. I never wanted to be separated from the love that we shared. Then life happened. We had children, we had careers, we had bills to pay, struggles to face, hard aches to overcome, sickness and even death muddied up the beauty of perfect love. While reading the Song of Solomon I find myself rewinding my own life and reminiscing of the love I once knew. Then the Holy Spirit spoke to me and told me that love still remains. It never wandered off; the devil just used life to cloud the picture a little bit.

God wants us to enjoy the love we have as couples. He made us for relationships. From the very beginning God knew that it was not good for man to be alone, so he created woman. Genesis 2:24 says, "Therefore shall a man leave his father and his mother, and shall cleave unto his wife: and they shall be one flesh." We are meant to have a bond between husband and wife that is romantic, loving, compassionate, understanding, and spiritually led in our relationships with Christ as well. Not only does The Song of Solomon remind me of the love between my wife and I, but it also stirs my heart of the affection that our Lord has for us. He created the world for us and gave us all the wonderful blessings that we enjoy. One of the greatest gifts he gave us is the loving bond a couple has, and it was done so that we were not physically alone, and that we would be stronger together. Oh, how our God loves us! In reading about the love and affection between King Solomon and his wife, I found myself experiencing the Love of God in a way that I never imagined. I realize that God's love for us is so much greater than anything we could ever read, write, or try to explain with mere words. As the hymn says, "The love of God is greater far, then tongue or pen could ever tell. It goes beyond the highest star and reaches to the deepest hell" (Lehman, 1917).

After wondering so many years why Song of Solomon is in the Bible, I am now very thankful God knew we would need to read this too. As I think of my wife while writings this, I am so glad that God gave me my "Rose of Sharon" in this life. As we walk through the twists and turns in this world may we always be reminded of the pure love Jesus has towards us. And may we remember that regardless of the situation or circumstances we find ourselves in, Christ is with us. We should always be able to see that clearly.

Read the Song of Solomon

- I know this is a strange request but take time to read through the "Song of Solomon" in its entirety.

- o God doesn't make mistakes, and there is a reason for this book in our Bible.
- If you are married, remind yourself of how you felt when you first met and fell in love with your husband or wife.
  - o Recall that love that you each had for one another.
  - o If the fire has died out, rekindle it in sincerity.
- And whether you are married or not, this week rekindle the fire you have for your first love, who is Jesus.
  - o Remember that He loved you so much that He died, so that you can Live forever.
  - o Get that passion back for Christ and let it pour out of you everywhere you go.
- Pray for God to redirect your heart back to Jesus and make Him first in your life.
  - o Your husband or wife should be second, not first; that position is reserved for the Lord!
- Journal this week how the "Song of Solomon" impacted you.
  - o What did you take away from it?

THE EXPECTATION OF THE WICKED

If you are like most people, you might wonder why there is so much evil in the world and why it seems to be getting worse. Every day the news media promotes the utter deterioration of our society by the sinless acts of violence, terror, murder, rape, robbery, and every other sin imaginable. We see it and it begins to wear on the hearts of even the righteous. Yes, sin seems to sell, and the world is buying at record levels. We are fascinated by the evil actions of others across the globe so much so that we stir the pot of the wicked through social media platforms in order to see what other evil may prevail because of it. Yes, our actions can cause others to fall into a sinful trap also. Stirring the pot of evil is also evil. It is almost as if the world has lost hope altogether. It is as if evil will continue to reign, and the wicked will prosper. But we know better. We know the truth from God's own Word, and regardless of how things appear at the moment, this will not end well for the dreadful in spirit.

Proverbs 10:28 says, "The hope of the righteous shall be gladness: but the expectation of the wicked shall perish." For those of us who are saved by the grace of God through the blood of Jesus, our hope is not in this present world. We need to take our eyes off the world around us and put our eyes continually on our Savior. We have a hope that is eternal, and salvation is nearer now than yesterday. But as for the evil doers, the ones who have sought to follow the god of this world, they shall expire. The Bible tells us that the expectation of the wicked shall perish, and we know that all who follow after the devil and his demonic forces shall face the same judgement and be cast into the lake of fire. But what about today? What are we to do at the moment? How should we overcome the wickedness of the world we live in right now? The answer is simple; we trust in God and do what He tells us to do.

In Psalm 112 we are told "Blessed is the man that feareth the Lord, that delighteth greatly in his commandments" (Psalm 112:1). It goes on to say that we shall not be moved, and that our hearts are fixed and established, trusting in the Lord. As a born-again Christian we know that this world is not our home, and that the devil and his angels are having a moment. We know there is wickedness, and that wickedness will continue on earth until the Lord calls the church home. But we can overcome the evil in this dark world by being the only light remaining. In Psalm 112, verse nine, the Word of God says that we are to give to the poor and that our righteousness shall endure. Why should we remain steadfast in the love of God even in the face of the ungodly? Because "The wicked shall see it and be grieved; he shall gnash with his teeth and melt away: the desire of the wicked shall perish" (Psalm 112:10). It could be that your good doings turn the hearts of the sinful man towards the Lord.

Do not grow weary of well doing brothers and sisters. The wicked will see it, and they will either repent and be saved or face the expectation that comes with wickedness, which is death. Be encouraged by the Lord this day and be a blessing to others so that your good works can be seen and glorify your father who is in heaven. Even in these last days, we are a city on a hill, the salt of the earth and the light of the world. Do not let your heart be troubled by what we know is happening around us, because we also know what is yet to come. May you all be blessed and be a blessing through Christ Jesus.

Read Proverbs 10:28, Psalm 7:11, 9:5, 9:16-17, 37:28,38.

- Just reading the wisdom from the scriptures provided we see the expected end for the wicked.
    - This is God's Word, not the words of mankind.
- Knowing that we all have an expected end, the wicked to destruction and the righteous to life everlasting, how does this change your approach to living your life?
- How does this knowledge change your approach to spreading the Gospel?
    - Does it put a burden on your heart to see others saved?

- When life gets you down and you are being persecuted by those who act wickedly, understand that you are not alone.
  - o We all receive that persecution from time to time.
- But also, take time to pray for that person or group that is persecuting. The Lord hears and it may be that your prayers are answered by the turning of their hearts as well.
  - o Also, if given the opportunity be nice to them in return, even offering them the Gospel.
  - o **Proverbs 25:21-22** *"If thine enemy be hungry, give him bread to eat; and if he be thirsty, give him water to drink: For thou shalt heap coals of fire upon his head, and the LORD shall reward thee."*
- Pray that God will use to touch the lives of even those that may appear to be wicked with the Gospel of Jesus.
- This week go out of your way to be nice to someone who mistreated you. It could just open the door for salvation for them.
- Journal your experiences throughout the week and see how God has opened doors and used you for His glory.

ARE YOU A STUMBLING BLOCK?

The Apostle Paul has a lot to say regarding our freedoms as Christians in his letters throughout the New Testament. He should know something about liberty. After all, Paul found liberty in knowing Christ who released him from the bonds of sin when he was still known as Saul of Tarsus. As Saul, he was persecuting Christians because he was a devout Jew who detested anything that gave the appearance of blasphemy to Judaism. At the time he was unaware that Christ was indeed the Messiah. He only realized that when Christ blinded him to the world and revealed Himself to Saul. Then there was a transformation in Saul's life that led to Saul becoming the Apostle to the Gentiles. We now know him as Paul, writer of thirteen letters found in the New Testament. As an Apostle of Christ, he planted churches and gave instruction to new converts to help them understand how they should behave and grow in their walk with Jesus as members of one body in Christ. We, as Christians today, are to study these books in the Bible and apply the lessons to our own lives. However, it is evident in observing our world today, that many of us have disregarded the truth of God's Word in the Bible and traded it for the lies of the world.

When Christians in Corinth were concerned about buying and consuming meats that came from animals offered unto pagan gods, Paul reminds them that you are not any better or worse off by eating the meat or refusing to eat the meat. It was not the act of eating the meat that was sinful, but it depended upon the heart of the one who ate it or restrained themselves from it. He says, "For every creature of God is good, and nothing is to be refused, if it be received with thanksgiving:" in 1 Timothy 4:4. But to the Corinthians he says, "but take heed lest by any means this liberty of yours become a stumbling block to them that are weak" (1 Corinthians 8:9). To the Romans, Paul writes, "It is good neither to eat flesh, nor to drink wine, nor anything whereby thy brother stumbleth, or is offended, or is made weak" (Romans 14:21). Although Paul is writing specifically about consuming food, we can apply this same lesson to our everyday lives today about anything that is offensive to others. Refraining from displaying something in front of others does not make you more of a Christian and it does not make you less of a Christian. However, it may keep your brother or sister in Christ from stumbling.

But we today are often stumbling blocks unaware because of our foolish pride. Jesus tells us to "Go ye therefore, and teach all nations, baptizing them in the name of the Father, and of the Son, and of the Holy Ghost" (Matthew 28:19). It is hard to do these things that Christ commands us to do if we are a stumblingblock before we even approach them. Everyone is different. We appear different, we act differently, we have different upbringing from home to home, and we even have cultural barriers within the same communities in which we live. Just because you feel a specific way about something does not mean someone else feels that specific way about it. We will never be able to reach the masses with the message of the gospel if we place our personal beliefs above our Christian convictions. The Word of God instructs us in how we should live, yet many today are justifying their actions based on historical events and the perception of things to come because of those historical events.

The fact is our freedom in Christ should make us stronger and not need to lean on worldly views. We should focus solely on Jesus and His Word rather than our own thoughts. This should apply to every situation and every day. Think about it; when Saul became Paul by way of knowing the truth, did he preach the gospel mixed in with Judaism? Did he behave as a Christian or did he behave as the world? Was he a light or was he a stumbling block? In the same way, we should not justify our old selves simply because that is who we were. And we should not mix our old selves in with the new creation in which we have become. The Bible says, "We then that are strong ought to bear the infirmities of the weak, and not to please ourselves" (Romans 15:1). We should be focused on strengthening our fellow brothers and sisters in Christ and not be a stumbling block to them.

Read 1 Timothy 4:4-5, 1 Corinthians 8:1-13, Romans 14:13-23, Romans 15:1-7

- We Christians are justified by faith, not by works (see Romans 3:28).
- We have freedom by our faith, but we should use this freedom to sin willfully (see Galatians 5:13).
  - o In fact, there are many who profess Christ that willingly embark in sinful activities, and in doing so, they are an offense.
  - o They are offensive to other believers.
  - o And they are an offense to the advancement of the Gospel.
    - If there is no difference between you and the world, then why would anyone of the world need the Gospel?
- How do you live knowing you have liberty being justified by faith in Christ Jesus?
- Pray for the lord to show you any area where you might be an offense to others and ask Him to take those offenses from you.
- Focus this week on not being a stumbling block to others within the faith, or an offense to the lost who might otherwise have come to faith in Christ Jesus.
- Write in you journal how these scriptures have impacted you and how you may or may not have modified your activities because of God's Word.

STRONGER TOGETHER

After the death of Joshua, the children of Israel cried to God for another leader asking who will lead them against the Canaanites. In the book of Judges, we see that God tells them that the tribe of Judah will be the one that God will deliver the land unto. Quickly Judah calls upon the tribe of Simeon. Together they are successful when they were in battle against the Canaanites. The House of Joseph also prevailed; but we must remember that the house of Joseph consisted of the tribes of Manasseh and Ephraim. In contrast, when the tribes of Benjamin, Manasseh, Ephraim, Zebulun, Asher, Naphtali, and Dan fought alone they were unsuccessful. Because these individual tribes were unsuccessful in their mission, the pagan people of Canaan continued to dwell amongst the children of Israel in the promised land, against the will of God. But the Angel of the Lord spoke to the Children of Israel; "And ye shall make no league with the inhabitants of this land; ye shall throw down their alters: but ye have not obeyed my voice: why have you done this? Wherefore I also said, I will not drive them out from before you: but they shall be as thorns in your sides, and their gods shall be a snare unto you" (Judges 2:2-3). As we examine the remainder of the Bible, we see that this is indeed the case. The children of Israel intermingle their faith, follow false, pagan gods, and the Lord Jehovah uses the surrounding nations to discipline His chosen people; even allowing them to be taken captive yet again.

It is no secret that God has blessed America as a nation. Once established on the foundations of the Bible and godliness we have gone the same direction of the Israelites. The difference with the Christian people of the United States is that we have invited in paganism and cultures that seek to destroy anything remotely Christian. Yes, we are a product of our own demise. We not only forgot the ways of our forefathers; we now have distain for them. As we look around our nation today, we see the deterioration of Christianity and the embracing of the numerous false gods in our lives. Our nation longs to exalt themselves above God and continues to crucify Jesus daily with the manner in which we live.

But there is good news. God has always left a remnant of believers. And that remnant, if joined together in faithful prayer and unity, will succeed where individuals have once failed. Just as Judah called upon Simeon and the house of Joseph was unified with Manasseh and Ephraim, Christians can help restore our nation to Christianity once gain. But we cannot do it alone. We have to lean on God through collective, faithful, and fervent prayer. We have allowed the voice of a few to distort the voice of Christ and His Church. Let us walk with Christ daily and let it be seen by your neighbor. Let the voice of the Lord be heard in your speech and let the love of God be seen in your actions. Let us so walk together publicly, denouncing the paganistic views of this world and once again promote Christian values and put Christ back in our lives, our homes, our communities, our schools, our courthouses and yes, our government. We are one nation under God and indivisible. But if we continue to let the pagan world dictate our country's direction, we will not stand. God will not bless the nation that has forsaken Him.

The Bible says, "If my people, which are called by my name, shall humble themselves, and pray, and seek my face, and turn from their wicked ways; then will I hear from heaven, and will forgive their sin, and will heal their land" (2 Chronicles 7:14). God is still talking to us today through His Holy Word in the Bible. If we would only listen and do what the Lord requires of us. We cannot worry about the actions of others if we ourselves are not doing what we have been called to do.

How do we expect others to come to Christ, when we which are of the Body of Christ do not walk according to His Word? We cannot see the revival in our land without first seeking revival in our own hearts. Those of us who believe on the name of the Lord Jesus, need to address ourselves, and then come together for the glory of the Lord, for His honor, praise, and glory. Let us remind the nation that there are more believers in Christ than those who wish to destroy the Church. Through Christ Jesus, we are stronger together.

Read Judges Chapter 2, 2 Chronicles 7:14, Psalm 33:12

- We can learn a lot as the New Testament Church from reading the history of God's people in the Old Testament.
- Do you think God blessed the United Sates as a nation?
- Do you think God is blessing us now as the nation continues to push Him away and move further from His Word?
- Christians are stronger when we ban together in prayer!
- This Week make it a priority to pray for our nation as a whole.
  o The people, the government, and the churches within our borders.
- However, before we can expect to see any change in the public, there must be evidence of Christ in us as individuals. Revival starts with you and me as individuals.
  o If you want a nation of Christians, then lead the way.
- Journal any observations you may have made this week that were Godly and ungodly. Compare and contrast your findings and pray that God would revive us once more.

WHO ARE YOU SEEKING?

In the first chapter of second Kings, we find Ahaziah is the King of Israel. He is the son of the wicked King Ahab and Jezebel. As we read, we discover that Ahaziah has fallen through a lattice, and he is in bad shape physically and very worried about his recovery. But he does not seek help from the hand of God, who brought the Hebrew people out of captivity in Egypt and has blessed them with the land in which they dwell. The Bible says, he sent messengers "and said unto them, go, enquire of Baalzebub the god of Ekron whether I shall recover of this disease" (2 Kings1:2). For those who do not know, Baalzebub is a major demonic force who was worshipped by Ekron, but also is a Philistine god and is associated with the Canaanite god Baal. So, the King of Israel, is seeking guidance from a pagan god of a people not his own. He is not after the Word of the Lord, God of Abraham, Isaac, and Jacob, the one who spoke the world into existence. He is garnering the wisdom of a pagan god of an ungodly people. The result is not exactly what he wanted.

The Bible records that the messengers encounter the prophet Elijah, who received word from the angel of the Lord regarding this issue. Elijah tells them, "…Is it not because there is not a God in Israel, that ye go to enquire of Baalzebub the god of Ekron. Now therefore thus saith the Lord, thou shalt not come down from that bed on which thou art gone up, but shall surely die…" (2 Kings 1:3-4). The King sends a few captains to bring Elijah down from his hilltop, but God reigned down fire on the first two captains and their men (one hundred total), but the third captain pleaded for his life and the life of his men before Elijah. The Lord told Elijah it was ok to go with this man unto the King and speak. Elijah appears before King Ahaziah and tells him exactly what he told his messengers; that the King would die for seeking the aid of Baalzebub and not the Lord. And in fact, King Ahaziah does die according to what Elijah had spoken unto him.

This should be a wakeup call for us in America. As Christians in this nation, we have the one and only true God living in us, in the Holy Spirit. We are saved by the grace of God through the atoning blood of Jesus Christ, God's only begotten son. We have a relationship with our Lord that allows us to go with boldness in prayer to the throne and know that He hears our words and answers us according to His will. However, as I look around our nation, I see more turmoil as sin is waxing worse in our society. I see people abandoning faith in God for faith in government. People have forsaken the God of all things seen and unseen, for the god of this world. People are seeking refuge in the safety of man and his laws, rather than the Lord Jehovah and His laws. We have lost our way as a nation, and it seems as though we are seeking Baalzebub for guidance. And just like Ahaziah, our nation will die where it lies. That is unless we return to God as a country. God: The Lord who brought us to this land, and who has blessed us as he blessed Israel and their land.

The Apostle Paul warns us to not be unequally yoked with unbelievers in 2 Corinthians 6:14 but that is exactly what we have done as a people. Not only have we become yoked together with unbelievers, but we also celebrate it and change our laws to accommodate the ungodly. What a treacherous act we have committed. As Elijah warned Israel, I am warning America. As a humble servant of God, I implore every believer in Jesus Christ, to pray and seek God's wisdom through the Bible. I beseech Christians to vote for leaders that will serve the Lord, not themselves. I ask that the body of Christ write, telephone, email, and use every other form of communication to tell our leaders who we are and who we serve. No more shall we bow to the gods of this world. No more shall we seek the wisdom of Baalzebub.

We were not instructed to conform to the world. Jesus said, "Go ye therefore and teach all nations, baptizing them in the name of the Father, and of the Son, and of the Holy Ghost: Teaching them to observe all things whatsoever I have commanded you: and, lo, I am with you alway, even unto the end of the world. Amen" (Matthew 28:19). Rather than pleasing the world, let us get back to doing what Jesus told us to do. Remember He is with us always, unto the end of the world. At this time, who is it that you seek?

- **Read 2 Kings Chapter 1, Matthew 28:16-20, Romans 1:18-32, Galatians 1:10**
- As a Christian, who are you seeking to please?
  - o Is it God or is it man?
  - o We should all be seeking to please God rather than man.
  - o That is in our individual lives and as a nation.
- We cannot call ourselves Christian and then vote, elect and condone sinful acts, behavior, and laws.
- This week pray once again for our nation and for all believers to be strong in the faith and to exercise our faith publicly and in the manner in which we live and operate.
- Remember that just because a law is on the books condoning sin, you do not have to partake in that law.
  - o For example, just because marijuana is legal, doesn't mean you smoke it.
- Prayerfully live in a purposeful manner in which you honor God in your daily life regardless of what else is going on and journal your experiences that you encounter.

HE MADE A CHANGE

There are many people today proclaiming they are Christians who honestly are not. There are some who profess Christ, yet do not know the Jesus of the Holy Bible. Many say they are followers of Jesus but have no idea the direction Jesus is leading. Now before anyone calls me out for being judgmental understand this; Jesus said "Beware of false prophets, which come in sheep's clothing, but inwardly they are ravening wolves. Ye shall know them by their fruits. Do men gather grapes of thorns, or figs of thistles? Even so every good tree bringeth forth good fruit, but a corrupt tree bringeth forth evil fruit" (Matthew 7:15-18). This is the very same chapter that just a few verses earlier he says, "judge not that ye be not judged" (Matthew 7:1). Jesus was not being contradictory; he was given us godly wisdom. He is telling the people judging that you need to fix yourselves before judging, because in the same manner you judge you will be judged. Then he tells us to watch out for false prophets who will be known by their fruit. In order to know a false prophet, we must first judge for ourselves. Jesus is not telling us not to judge, he is telling us to live righteously and use discernment (righteous judgement) regarding others.

In fact, discernment is a gift given by the Holy Spirit. The scriptures say, "But strong meat belongeth to them that are full of age, even those who by reason of use have their senses exercised to discern both good and evil" (Galatians 5:14). So, we know that Christians who are seeking the Lord and exercising their faith daily through prayer and study of God's Word, can have the gift of discernment. What is discernment? It is defined as "the ability to judge well" or "...to obtain spiritual guidance and understanding" (Online Dictionary, 2020). As one who studies the Bible, prays daily, and seeks God's wisdom it is easy to see identify false Christians from true believers and followers of Christ. It is easy, because I just look at their fruit; I see what they are doing and how they are living. I just make simple observations. Now I know there will be some who think that I am being holier than thou, and that is ok. I can manage the criticism because I just give it to God in prayer. It is true, I cannot see your heart or know your intentions, but I can see your labor or lack thereof for the Lord.

There is a gospel song I sometimes sing called "He Made a Change" that explains things in a biblical perspective. The first verse says in part; "When Paul met the Lord on Damascus Road, he never was the same again; When Peter met the Lord, he left his boat and started fishing for men" (Lindsey, n.d.). How true is this description of not only what happened to Peter and Paul and all of the Apostles, but what happens to a new believer in Christ. Jesus told Nicodemus, "...Verily, verily I say unto thee, except a man be born again, he cannot see the kingdom of God" (John 3:3). And when someone is truly born again, they have confessed their sins, asked for forgiveness with repentance (to turn away from wickedness) and received Jesus as their Lord and Savior. Then the Holy Spirit dwells in them.

And as Paul says a born-again believer is no longer the same; "Therefore if any man be in Christ, he is a new creature: old things passed away; behold, all things are become new" (2 Corinthians 5:17). In essence, a born-again believer in Christ is not the person they used to be. They have shed the old man and put on the new person created in Christ Jesus. It is Christ Jesus who makes the change in us when we come to him with true repentance and are saved by the grace of God. It is not that we become perfect humans, but are made perfect in Jesus our Lord, and grow daily in our walk with Christ.

We no longer behave as the world but walk in the ways and will of God. We strive to be better today than yesterday, and better tomorrow than today. A Christian is known for their walk, not by their talk alone. Christians can be identified because of the change that takes place in their heart. A child of God is changed. They are changed by their faith in Jesus, by their willingness to surrender their lives, and by the Holy Spirit who makes them a new creature. As the song lyrics continue it is as if it was written about me; "Now I may not be Peter or Paul, but one thing I can truly say; when I met the Lord and made him my choice,

He definitely made a change. He Made a Change!" Has the Lord made a change in you?

- **Read all of Matthew Chapter 7 (don't stop after verse 1), Galatians 5:14, John 3:1-21 & 2 Corinthians 5:11-21**
- How has Salvation changed you?
- Are you the same person you used to be, or are you growing daily in your walk with Jesus?
- Do you know anyone who says they are believers, but live like the world?
- Do you still go to the same old places you used to go and continue in the same old worldly and sinful things you used to before you were saved?
- Now that you have read all of Matthew 7, John 3:1-21 and 2 Corinthians 5:11-21 does "judge not" still mean the same to you?
- This week pray that God will continue to provide you the wisdom of His Word through the Holy Spirit and lean on His understanding and not your own.
- Also make a concerted effort to surrender to God and His Word, becoming more Christ like each day.
    o Remember, He makes the change, not us. But we have to be willing to allow Him to change us.
- Journal your experiences and record if you have noticed any differences in your everyday life as you continue to grow in your relationship with the Lord.

THE FLEEING DISCIPLES

In Mark Chapter 14, we read about the betrayal of Jesus Christ. We learn that as the closest followers of Christ sat at the Lord's table for his final meal during the feast of Passover and Unleavened Bread, that Jesus prophesied of one of his own betraying him. Immediately his followers become defensive and demand to know who it is among them that would do such a thing. All of them deny it could be them specifically. Jesus, keeping the prophesy of Zechariah 13:7 explained to his disciples that they all would be offended of Jesus that night. And while we today famously remember how Peter vehemently denies that he would ever be offended of Christ. We overlook what the scriptures say immediately following his proclamation to Jesus. The very last sentence in Mark 14:31 says, "...likewise also said they all." All the disciples echoed what Peter declared unto our Lord. It was not just Peter that made this bold statement. They all said they would not be offended by Jesus. They all were declaring their loyalty, faith, and allegiance unto the Messiah, whom they all walked with every day. And even though we all know that Jesus' prophesy of Peter denying Him thrice before the cock crew twice came to fruition, so did the fullness of Jesus' earlier prophesy from Zechariah 13:7.

After praying in the Garden of Gethsemane and chastising Peter, John, and James for falling asleep, Jesus was arrested. After receiving the kiss of death from Judas Iscariot, the multitude that were with him seized Jesus. But what happens next is quite alarming to me. The scripture says, "They all forsook him, and fled" (Mark 14:50). You see, it was not just Peter who forsook our Lord, it was all of the disciples. The followers of Jesus were constantly surrounding Him and praising his works when everything was going well for them. When Jesus was changing the water into wine, casting out demons, calming the storms, raising Lazarus from the dead, and healing the sick and injured, everyone was rejoicing with the Lord. Everyone wanted to be seen with Him and let the whole region know they were with Jesus. But the minute the tides turned, even though Jesus told them beforehand what would happen and that it must happen, they all fled. Everyone one of them turned the other way when it came down to life and death on earth. Thankfully, the apostles of Christ were all given a life to do service for the Lord after His death, but it took the physical resurrection for them to get their acts together. After his crucifixion, the followers of Jesus were distraught until they saw him as the risen Christ.

We as followers of Christ in the modern times seemed to have not learned very much from studying the scriptures. Because most probably do not study the scriptures at all. We have the wisdom of the Holy Spirit and the knowledge of the resurrection in the Word of God. Yet, many disciples (followers of Christ) today are doing the same thing. When times are good and going our way, we celebrate, congregate, and worship for the entire world to see. But the minute something bad happens or the tides shift, we see the present-day disciples of Jesus flee. Today, perhaps more than any other time in history, the church has come under persecution. The enemy has beguiled the masses into believing that the Christian Church is bigoted, prejudiced, and even racist because we follow the Word of God in the Holy Bible. Because of this modern viewpoint from the devil and his followers, many who have professed Christ have turned their back on Jesus and His church and have fled. The local churches are empty or have a miniscule congregation. Even before the COVID-19 crisis, the churches were losing worshipers. The Bible tells us to fear not and to know that He is Lord. The Bible tells us that God is with us wherever we go. God's Word also says, "Not forsaking the assembling of ourselves together, as the manner of some is; but exhorting one another: and so much the more, as ye see the day approaching" (Hebrews 10:25). The day is fast approaching friends. Are you going to stand with Jesus and keep His Word, or will we all forsake Him and become just another fleeing disciple?

- **Read all of Zechariah 13 (with a focus on verse 7), and all of Mark 14 (all 72 verses), and Hebrews 10:19–39 (focus on verse 25).**

- Do you attend your Church services regularly?
- What does Regularly mean to you?
- Is it once a week, once a month, or once a quarter?
- Do you know how many services your local Church offers?
- How many of those do you attend?
- When the doors are open, are you present?
- Do you meet with other believers outside of Church to pray and have Christian fellowship?
- Do people in your community know by looking at you and hearing you speak, that you belong to Christ?
- Focus your prayer this week on giving God thanks that you live in a free nation where you can worship Him openly without fear. And make it a point, if you don't already, to pray for your pastor and ministry leaders and for your Church as a whole.
- If you are not yet doing so, find a Bible believing Church and attend regularly.
- My definition of regular is when the doors are open, and you are able to attend.
- Journal this week making observations of those who you know are not ashamed of the Gospel, and that everyone knows they belong to Jesus. Make a mental note of how they live.

THANK GOD

People are in such a rush today. We hustle around trying to make sure that everything gets done exactly how we want it or need it to be. We get impatient if the internet does not load fast enough for us, or if the line at the drive through isn't moving along quickly. We get annoyed at the person waiting on us at the store because they aren't moving at the speed we would like them to, or perhaps we feel as though their attitudes aren't pleasant enough for our service. Yes, we tend to get "put out" by the smallest of things never truly realizing just how good we all have it. Afterall, we have been taught by the media and the current society that we live in, that if something is not to our liking, we should just throw a fit until somebody changes everything to suit us. If we do not get our way, we can just get louder. And if that does not work then we should resort to violence. Perhaps we can find a few more like-minded people and be violent together. Surely, we can find a way to get what we want!

How sad we have become. Everybody takes things for granted anymore, as if the world revolves around them and everybody is at their beck and call. It seems to me that most people alive on this earth have become so spoiled and self-centered that we never acknowledge just how blessed we are for the things we have. We are too busy being upset about what we do not have. The Bible says, "Give thanks unto the Lord; call upon his name: make known his deeds among the people" (Psalm 105:1). In all the clamoring for attention and demands for a better life, it sure would be nice to see God's children giving thanks to the Lord, for He is good, and His love endures forever!

The vocal minority have high-jacked our country and have managed to raise their ruckus to an all-time high so that everything else is drowned out. It sure would be nice to see and hear the praises of our Lord overcome the sadness and madness that has enveloped our nation. Let us think about this for a minute. As you read this, do you have a roof over your head? Are you clothed? Do you have food to eat? Are there people in your life who love you and care for you? Are you healthy or are you receiving medical care? Do you have a job? Do you have finances? Do you have groceries? Are you and your family being cared for in any way? If you answered yes to any of these questions, then you are blessed and have more than a lot of people in other parts of the world. I served in the military for a long time and served in many countries. I can tell you firsthand that Americans do not have it bad at all. The ones making the most noise today have never experienced true hardships, but if they continue to act as they are they will know these hardships all too well. Then they will realize just how good they really had it.

Let us as believers in Jesus set the example today as we walk with the Lord. Let us praise the Lord and be thankful for the blessings God has given us, not only as Christians, but as Americans living in this great country of ours. Rather than spew off at the mouth about how bad things have gotten or how bad things are, let us remind the world of how blessed we are as we sing God's praises and live the life Jesus called us to live, spreading the love of God and the gospel of Jesus Christ. Psalm 105 continues and says, "sing unto him, sing psalms unto him; talk ye of all his wonderous works. Glory ye in his Holy name: let the heart of them rejoice that seek the Lord" (Psalm 105:2-3).

If you know the Lord and seek after him, let your voice be heard on high. Let your praises to God drowned out the hatred and discontent that is so prevalent in today's culture. It could be that God uses your joy in the Lord and for the Lord to change the hearts of those who are disgruntled with the world. In that very same psalm, the Word of the Lord says, "And he increased his people greatly, and made them stronger than their enemies" (Psalm 105:24). Do not fall into the temptation to return evil with evil. Return love in the face of evil and sing the praises of our Lord. Regardless of your current situation, you are blessed, and God loves you so much that He sent His son to die for you so that you could live forever with Him (See John 3:16). Thank God!

- **Read Psalm 105, Psalm 136:1-3, Ephesians 2:8-9 & 1 Peter 2:9-10**
- Are you thankful for the free gift of salvation?
- Does the world know you are thankful unto God for salvation?
- Does God hear your thankfulness in your daily life?
- Make it point this week to begin to live a life of praise unto God deliberately.
- Jesus said in **Matthew 5:16** *"Let your light so shine before men, that they may see your good works, and glorify your Father which is in heaven."* So Let it SHINE!
- Take time this week to look up scriptures of praise unto the Lord and jot down a few of those in your journal.
- Pray that God will give you opportunities to shine your light for His glory before others.
- Journal this week how you have purposefully lived a life praising Jesus publicly and annotate any observations you may have noticed both positively and negatively.

CHARITY OF THE SAINTS

What do you think of when you think of the word "charity"? Merriam – Webster defines the term as, "generosity and helpfulness especially toward the needy or suffering, an institution engaged in relief of the poor, public provision for the relief of the needy, benevolent goodwill toward or love of humanity, a gift for public benevolent purposes, or an institution (such as a hospital) founded by such a gift" (Webster, 2020). However, as Christians, what do you know the word to truly mean? That may all depend on what you are reading. The Apostle Paul tells us exactly what Charity is in 1 Corinthians, chapter 13. However, "charity" is not mentioned in all versions of the Bible. The King James Bible clearly identifies the Greek word "agape" as "charity" in the English language.

Newer English versions of the Bible such as the New International Version (NIV) translate this word simply as "love." If you look up the definition for the English word "love" you will find something similar to the following: "strong affection for another arising out of kinship or personal ties, attraction based on sexual desire: affection and tenderness felt by lovers, affection based on admiration, benevolence, or common interests, an assurance of affection, or warm attachment, enthusiasm, or devotion" (Webster, 2020). Clearly there is a difference between mere love and genuine charity.

I have heard many preachers explain the word "love" as a much deeper word than how we have come to understand love to be. They spend a lot of time explaining that the word love in 1 Corinthians, chapter 13 comes from the Greek word "agape" and expresses a deeper commitment for others and is the same "love" Christ has towards us. They say something to the effect that it is not the human "love" we know but God's love. Exactly! And that is why the King James translators used the word "charity" when translating "agape." Because it is different and does not mean the same thing simply as "love." Why spend time in a sermon explaining that when the translators have already done it for us? Christ had charity toward us and gave himself for us. That is deeper than the love the world has come to know today. That is "agape" …that is "charity."

People today say they love, but when they become upset or disgruntled, they walk away. I am told that the divorce rate among married couples is more than 50% in the world today. That is not the charity that Paul writes about. The Greek word for that type of love would be "eros." "Eros is desire in search of satisfaction. Eros seeks its object in order to satisfy its own hunger. Eros seeks its object for the worth and value it has for its own self-fulfillment. Unlike agape, eros seeks its own" (Bible Gateway, 2020). In contrast, "Charity suffereth long, and is kind; charity envieth not; charity vaunteth not itself, is not puffed up, Doth not behave itself unseemly, seeketh not her own, is not easily provoked, thinketh no evil; Rejoiceth not in iniquity, but rejoiceth in the truth; Beareth all things, believeth all things, hopeth all things, endureth all things" (1 Corinthians 13:4-7).

The world's view of love has become lust and when one exchanges lust for love, it is simply to sow to the flesh and not to put the love of God before themselves. The world's view of love is "eros," a selfish desire to receive something that is beneficial to them. If that benefit no longer exists, then neither does the affection exist toward the other. No, "agape" is not simply "love." Agape is charity. Do you share the charity that Christ has toward us? Or are you simply loving as the world loves until it is no longer of any benefit to you? Remember we can have and do many things for the church, but it is charity that is held as the greatest; "And now abideth faith, hope, charity, these three; but the greatest of these is charity (1 Corinthians 13:13).

- **Read 1 Corinthians Chapter 13**
- What kind of love are you displaying towards your Church family, your blood family, and toward unbelievers?
- Do you have the agape love that is the charity of the Lord?
- Remember this isn't a onetime action. It is a way of life.

- This week look up the Greek words for love: Agape, Érōs, Philía, Philautía, **Storgē**, and Xenía.
- How does understanding the differences of the definition of these words, help you in regard to how you love God and your neighbor verses how you love your spouse and siblings?
- This week pray that God will lead you in the path of righteousness where you can demonstrate Charity towards others. Remember that we are His ambassadors and represent Him.
- Journal this week how this devotional has helped you better understand the love (Charity) of God towards us, and how it may have changed the way you demonstrate that towards others.

HALFWAY HOME

Congratulations! You are half-way through this fifty-two-week devotional and are still going strong. I applaud you as you continue to demonstrate your desire to devote time to God and the Study of His Word, growing in your relationship with Christ. I do so hope that you have learned and grown spiritually as you have journeyed this far. Many people begin devotional plans and end up falling by the wayside due to a variety of reasons. So, kudos to you for driving through the mire of life and staying focused and on task with this book. I encourage you to continue on this journey.

By now you have realized that this is not your usual devotional of reading a paragraph, looking at one verse of scripture, and checking the block. This devotional book actually was derived from articles that I wrote for our local paper and was intended to make people think, open their Bibles and study for themselves. It was intended to get the attention of the unbelievers and believers alike. When these were published in the paper, I received numerous emails, and text messages from believers. Some were encouraging and some were a little less than encouraging.

While I realize that not everyone is going to respond the same way, and some may even take offense to what I have written, I do hope and pray that people will take the time to prayerfully study the Bible for themselves as I stated in the introduction. This is not about winning an argument or having people like me or showering me with accolades. My intent is to get people to study the Word of God as individuals and lean on the Holy Spirit of God for guidance rather than a man or woman. And that includes me. You have come this far, so I assume that you are doing just that.

As you continue on with the reading plan, I hope and pray that you are being led by the Spirit of God and that you are developing a deeper, more meaningful relationship with the Lord. I pray that your relationship is evident in your life. Because often times our life speaks louder than our words, our life needs to mirror that of Jesus and His Word. If we talk the talk, let us also walk the walk. Do not get discouraged when you stumble. As I have said before, give it to the Lord in prayer and get back up and back at it. I pray the Lord continues to lead you and bless you and makes you a blessing to others you have contact with. We had a saying in the military; "Lean forward in the foxhole". I encourage you to Keep leaning forward!

FARTHER ALONG

The old Hymn says, "Farther along we'll know about it; farther along, we'll understand why." As Christians we do not fully understand everything that is taking place on earth. We can look all around us and get consumed by the evil deeds of mankind and the wickedness that is erupting every waking moment, but it will do us not one bit of good. The Apostle Paul says, "For now we see through a glass, darkly; but then face to face: now I know in part; but then shall I know even as also I am known" (1 Corinthians 13:12). You and I only know a fraction of what is going on. We truly only see a minute portion of the big picture. Yet we often tend to let this little bit we know disrupt our lives. We seem to only dwell on the negativity that surrounds us as if it is this great chasm that will destroy us all. This ought not to be for the believer in Christ.

If you are a believer in Jesus, then you know this is not all there is. You know there is more to come. Jesus said, "Let not your heart be troubled: ye believe in God, believe also in me. In my Father's house are many mansions: if it were not so, I would have told you. I go to prepare a place for you. And if I go and prepare a place for you, I will come again, and receive you unto myself; that where I am, there ye may be also" (John 14:1-3). What a beautiful promise that God has given us as followers of Jesus. So, while things down here on earth may look troublesome, we should smile and hold our heads up knowing that our redeemer lives, and that He has prepared a place for us. And what is more, He is coming back very soon to take us home. Why should we walk around with a troubled heart when we know that we will all be in Glory with Jesus? Friends, we should not. Do not walk with your head down. Look up because our redeemer draweth nigh (see Luke 21:28).

You must also remember that non-believers are watching us. We are in fact Ambassadors of Christ. We are earthly representatives of Jesus. As such we should present ourselves in a fashion that displays the truthfulness of our blessing. We are saved from eternal damnation by the grace of God the Father through the atoning blood of God the Son and we live with God the Holy Spirit indwelling in us. We have the Truth, and the Truth has indeed made us free. We are free from the bondage of sin, and we are free from the misery of this life. Because we know that the Trumpet of the Lord shall sound, and the voice of the Archangel will be heard, and we will all be caught up together in the clouds to be with the Lord forever (see 1 Thessalonians 4:13-18).

Ambassadors should be positive representatives, not negative onlookers. The world around us may be waxing cold and evil is becoming brazen, but this was foretold to us to help us understand the seasons. We shall overcome because our Savior has already overcome. Everything He has told us in His Word has either already happened, or soon will happen. That is something to be joyful about. Just this week I heard a preacher say, "Things are looking pretty good, because things are looking pretty bad" (Smith, 2020). That is something for us to think about!

Yes, things look bleak at the moment. But things are not falling apart. Things are falling into place. Things are happening just as the Bible has told us they would. And while we should be on fire for the Lord and spreading the gospel to everyone out of genuine concern for others eternity, we should also take solace in the fact that our eternity is already secured. We may not fully understand the reasoning for everything that is taking place right now, but farther along we will understand why. So, cheer up my brothers and sisters and live in the sunshine. We will understand it all by and by.

- **Read 1 Corinthians 13:12, John 14:1-3, Luke 21:28 and Thessalonians 4:13-18**
- **Also look up the lyrics to the Hymn: "Farther Along"**
- Does knowing the truth of God's Promises in the Bible help you live more confidently even though the world around us seems to be falling apart?
- When you get discouraged, do you turn to God in prayer and seek out His promises in scripture?

- I encourage you this week to spend more time in the Bible than you do watching the News.
- However, as you watch the News and observe the things around you, take solace in the fact that Jesus has already prepared a place for you, and he is coming back to get us soon.
- This week, start walking with the confidence and authority of a believer in Christ. Not in arrogance but in the confidence of the Lord, knowing that when all is said and done, we shall be with Jesus in glory!
- Journal your thoughts about knowing the promises of God and give Him all thanks and praise for what He has done, is doing and is about to do.

FORSAKE NOT GOD'S PRECEPTS

The psalmist writes, "They had almost consumed me upon earth; but I forsook not thy precepts" (Psalm 119:87). Just a few verses earlier he exclaims to the Lord that evil is all around him and his enemies are executing judgment against him, and that he is living under continuous persecution. Yet, the psalmist cries out, "I do not forget thy statutes" (Psalm 119:83). This is an incredibly good passage to learn from in the age we are living in now. Under the current climate in the United States, we can see Christians beginning to be persecuted publicly for our faith in Jesus Christ and our unwavering knowledge of the truth in the Holy Bible.

During the COVID-19 Pandemic some states outlawed attendance or singing praises to God while attending services. Churches were being burned in parts of the country by non-believers who were disgusted at the fact that Christians continued to assemble during a pandemic. There was a protest in Portland, Oregon where people gathered in the streets to burn the Bible and the American flag together. No matter how this was spun, it had nothing to do with the death of a George Floyd in Minnesota but had everything to do with the death of Christianity in America and death to the America that stands for Jesus. This was and still is an all-out assault on Jesus and his followers, and it is being led by Satan himself. You may see faces and hear voices from various people, and some may even be elected officials, but the thoughts and intents are coming from the devil.

We Christians can relate to the psalmist as we seem to be encompassed by enemies of our faith. It had even gotten to the point where some believers have gone into hiding or in retreat mode. Some Christians were staying home, and some were avoiding the public altogether. Churches were and, in many cases, still empty or only partially filled on Sunday and Wednesday evenings. Many pointed to the COVID-19 crisis for staying away, yet the truth of the matter is that the numbers were dwindling even before March 2020. We should not be afraid or worrisome about the current climate regarding faith, but we should be worried about the lack of standing firm in our faith in Jesus at a time of worldly uncertainty.

This is a truth; the world may look uncertain, but faith in Jesus Christ is not uncertain at all. We have a blessed hope and an expectation of the Promise of eternal life with Christ. We know that Jesus is waiting for the Father to say bring them home, and at that point we will join Jesus while the world deals with the antichrist and his regime for seven years. Since we know the truth, why are we not shouting it from the rooftops? Why are we not keeping God's precepts in the face of adversity? Why have we abandoned our responsibilities as disciples of Christ just because the public does not accept us anymore? Now more than ever, we need to be assembling for worship and make our presence known in public for the glory of God. The Bible says, "Let us hold fast the profession of our faith without wavering; (for he is faithful that promised;) And let us consider one another to provoke unto love and to good works: Not forsaking the assembling of ourselves together, as the manner of some is; but exhorting one another: and so much the more, as ye see the day approaching" (Hebrews 10:23-25).

Shadrach, Meshack and Abednego would not bow down and worship the idol of Nebuchadnezzar when the music played. Even though it meant they would be placed in the furnace, they refused to dishonor God Almighty. And as the song says, they would not bend, they wouldn't bow, and they wouldn't burn. God protected them in the fiery furnace! The same God that protected them, protects you and me. We should be like the three Hebrew boys just as they told King Nebuchadnezzar, even if God does not save us, we will not bow to your idol. However, a lot of us today have already bowed down to the idol that our state and local governments have placed before us.

Now as we look around our nation, the Body of Christ is surrounded by those who wish to inflict persecution upon us, and even eliminate the church altogether. I cannot speak for the entirety of the Church. I can only speak for myself and attempt to influence others through faith in Jesus. However, I am and will continue to be like the psalmist. The antagonists of the church may be all around me, but I will not forsake God's precepts. I will pray to God anywhere I desire to pray. I will worship God anywhere and at any time I desire to worship. I will read and study God's Word daily, and I will follow where he leads and do what He tells me to do. I will be at the house of worship, singing praises to the Lord, and I will hear his Word preached at the appointed times.

- **Read Daniel Chapter 3, Psalm 119:83-87 (I recommend you read the entire Psalm) & Hebrews 10:23-25 again.**
- When you read the story of Shadrach, Meshack and Abednego in Daniel Chapter 3, do you get encouraged by their faithfulness, or do you view this simply as a "story"?
    - o I remind you that all of God's Word is Truth.
- In the world we live in today, do other people's ideals and convictions deter you from openly worshipping God in a Biblical manner?
- How does what the Bible says about our faith rejuvenate you to openly worship Christ?
- This week, make it a focal point to openly worship God. We don't have to jump in people's faces, but we don't have to coward down and hide either. Our faith is just as important as their lack of faith. In fact, it is more important.
- Pray and ask God to strengthen you in your faith to stand even in the face of oppression to worship our Lord and Savior, Jesus Christ.
- Don't forget to journal your experiences this week.
    - o Did you notice how society influences Christians?
    - o Are Christians visible or less visible today?
    - o Or do you think more Christians are keeping to themselves?

THY SERVANT HEARETH

In studying the Old Testament book of 1 Samuel chapter three, I came across a phrase that I believe would be greatly beneficial to everyone today. The Priest, Eli, gives the young prophet to be, Samuel, a directive after Samuel continues to interrupt Eli's sleep. On three separate occasions on this particular night Samuel heard a voice calling unto him and he thought it was the priest, Eli. However, after the third time of being awakened, Eli realizes it must be the Lord calling Samuel and Samuel did not recognize it. So, in verse nine Eli gives the young Samuel the best advice anyone can give; Eli says, "Go lie down: and it shall be, if he call thee, that thou shalt say, Speak, Lord; for thy servant heareth" (1 Samuel 3:9). The young Samuel does just that. When he heard the voice call out to him again, he replied, "Speak; for thy servant heareth" (1 Samuel 3:10).

This passage got me to wondering about my past, and just how many times the Lord called unto me that I did not either hear, recognize, or flat out ignored Him. In reflecting I can identify many times in my life that God was calling me. Sometimes the noise around me was so loud that I did not hear the soft and gentle whisper of the Lord. Other times, as I look back, I could hear him but did not know enough about the Word of God to understand that it was Him speaking to me. Instead, I went the way of the world because, again, the world's voice was louder to me at the time. And then of course, there were many times that I knew God was calling me and I willingly chose not to listen. Therefore, I am guilty of ignoring His voice altogether. I thank God that His voice got louder and rose above the noise threshold of the world that I placed in my life. But I often wonder how different my life would have been and what kind of positive impact I could have had on other people, most importantly my children, if I had just listened to God's call earlier in my life. I have no doubt I am where I need to be today because God's timing is perfect. But it still makes me wonder and sometimes I am filled with shame due to my lack of responding to God earlier in my life.

The Lord used Samuel mightily as a prophet to his people and he can use you mightily for His glory as well if you will listen to Him calling out to you. I implore you to open up the Bible and read it. I beseech you to turn down the noise threshold that is surrounding you right now and listen to that still soft voice. You will be amazed at what He tells you and just how He will lead you. The Bible says that God will never leave you nor forsake you (see Hebrews 13:5). For many years I did what I wanted to do, when I wanted to do it without regard to listening to God and without regard to how that impacted other people's lives. I am a witness to the grace, mercy, and love of Christ Jesus today and can tell you firsthand that God has mighty things in store for you. But you will never know what they are if you are not listening to Him speak to you. If you continue to have the noise of the world turned up so loud that you neglect to hear God's voice you are going to miss out on His blessings in your life on earth and the many rewards that await us in heaven.

If you are reading this right now, I want you to know that it is not a mistake. I want you to know that God is calling you right at this moment. The Lord Jesus gave his life so that we can have eternal life with Him forever in glory and be free from the condemnation that faces non-believers in the lake of fire. Listen to His voice. Turn off the noise of the world. Pray earnestly and fervently to God and cry out to Him today. Adhere to the advice given to Samuel from the priest Eli. Allow God to speak to your heart and listen to what He tells you. Pray and read your Bible daily so that you will know what His perfect plan is for you. Learn from God himself and not from the world. Spend time with Him and allow Him to move in your life and use you for His glory. Listen and say, "Speak Lord; Thy Servant Heareth."

- **Read 1 Samuel Chapter 3, Hebrews 13:5, 1 Thessalonians 5:24, 1 Peter 1:15 & John 12:27–35**
- How does it feel knowing that you are called by God?
- Does knowing you are called by God change the way you interact with others on a daily basis?

- Do you use your calling by Grace through faith in Jesus as a springboard to glorify God or do you keep salvation and God's glory to yourself?
- Pray that God will constantly remind you that you were called and called for a purpose, which is to share the Gospel of Jesus and glorify Him with your life.
- Record in your journal this week how knowing you were called out of the world into the glorious Gospel and for the Gospel shapes who you are and how you behave daily.
- Do you see this calling on others in your life?

CRUCIFIED, BAPTIZED, CLOTHED & RAISED

I do not know whether it is the times we live in or not, but I am noticing more people who call themselves Christians living as if they are not. Now some reading this might think that I am being very judgmental and even a little legalistic in my viewpoint. Afterall, the Bible clearly says that "For whosoever shall call upon the name of the Lord shall be saved" (Romans 10:13) and it also clearly states, "That if thou shalt confess with thy mouth the Lord Jesus, and shalt believe in thine heart that God hath raised him from the dead, thou shalt be saved" (Romans 10:9). This is the truth and about that there is no doubt. Anyone who calls on the name of the Lord Jesus Christ and believes in their heart is saved and it is done instantly.

So, why am I so judgmental when it comes to seeing people live as the world? The answer is simple; worldly people are worldly and not of the Kingdom of God. I am concerned about their eternity and want them to be sure of where they are going. As a Christian I am commanded to preach the gospel to everyone (see Mark 16:15) and I am commanded to love the Lord my God with everything that I am and all that I have and to love my neighbor as myself (see Matthew 22:37-39). I would not be a very loving person if I simply sat back and watched people go to hell because they believed the lie that Satan has whispered in their ears. You see, we as Christians are bought with a price and are no longer our own when we become born-again in the Spirit (see 1 Corinthians 6:20 & 7:23).

While the Bible clearly states what one must do to be saved from the condemnation that awaits sinners in hell and ultimately the Lake of Fire, the Bible is also very clear on who we are in Christ and who we are with Christ. The Apostle Paul had a lot to say on these matters of life and death. Paul states, "I am crucified with Christ: nevertheless I live; yet not I, but Christ liveth in me: and the life which I now live in the flesh I live by the faith of the Son of God, who loved me, and gave himself for me" (Galatians, 2:20). So, who we once were is no longer present. We have been crucified with him and therefore the old person we used to be is dead and buried. Yet we still live but it is not really us anymore, it is Christ living in us and we now live by faith in Jesus and are free from the world of sin.

Paul also says, "For as many of you as have been baptized into Christ have put on Christ" (Galatians 3:27). A born-again believer has removed the old filthy rags of our sinful nature and have put on the new creature in Christ. When people see us, they should see Christ and not the old you and me. You see, we have been buried and the sinful nature that existed in us has been destroyed and is buried also. Paul tells the Colossians, "If ye then be risen with Christ, seek those things which are above, where Christ sitteth on the right hand of God. Set your affection on things above, not on things on the earth. For ye are dead, and your life is hid with Christ in God" (Colossians 3:1-3).

You might be thinking, what does Paul know? Considering he was chosen by our Lord and Savior, Jesus Himself, and that he wrote thirteen letters (14 counting Hebrews) found in the New Testament, I would say he knows a lot. His letters make around fifty percent of the New Testament, which is the basis and foundation of the Christian faith. I remind you that the Bible says, "All scripture is given by inspiration of God, and is profitable for doctrine, for reproof, for correction, for instruction in righteousness:" (1 Timothy 3:16).

We either believe it all or none of it. We cannot simply say I believe the parts where I am saved by grace and then turn around and disregard the rest of God's Word. If you are a born-again Christian, saved by the grace of God through faith in Jesus Christ, then you have put off the old man. You have been crucified with Him, baptized by Him, clothed in Him, and raised in truth and righteousness in Christ Jesus. You are an ambassador of heaven. Or at least you should have done these things. Do not set your eyes on earthly things, but on the things above. Do not live for the world, live for Christ, and walk by the Spirit.

- **Read Romans 10:13, Mark 16:15, Matthew 22:27-39, 1 Corinthians 6:20 & 7:23, Galatians 2:20 & 3:27, Colossians 3:1-3 and 1 Timothy 3:16**
- Have you lived your life as a believer up to this point knowing that you were bough with the price of the precious blood of Jesus Christ?
- Do you know that you are not your own?
- Have you crucified your old self and put on the new man created in the righteousness of Jesus Christ?
- Pray that God will continue to transform you by the renewing of your mind to be more like Christ and less like the world or the old you.
- Make it focal point this week to let the new creation be seen among everyone you encounter.
- Journal your thoughts on the scriptures we have read in the Word of God and list anything that you have noticed where the old you is gone and the new you is present.

LET US REASON TOGETHER

In my discussions with people over the last few years regarding salvation through knowing Jesus Christ as Lord and Savior, I have had many people tell me that they do not think there can be a God who truly loves us. Some people even go as far as to say that If God really existed and was truly a loving father, how could he permit such evil to exists in the world. They go on to say how could a loving God condone global disasters, murders, diseases, rapist, and all the evil that is so prevalent in the world today. My answer is a plain one. He does not condone it at all. God is against the evil that is prevalent in our society. The Bible says, 'These six things doth the LORD hate: yea, seven are an abomination unto him: A proud look, a lying tongue, and hands that shed innocent blood, An heart that deviseth wicked imaginations, feet that be swift in running to mischief, A false witness that speaketh lies, and he that soweth discord among brethren" (Proverbs 6:16-19).

Does that sound like God likes or condones wickedness and evil? The fact is that the devil has entered into the picture and has been enticing man to do the exact opposite of God's will since the garden of Eden. And sadly, man has not learned from His sinful past and continues to live in a sinful nature of pleasing his flesh without regard to the righteousness of God and His directives to his greatest creation, humanity. Because man chose to listen to Satan and his lies, we became a fallen creature and live in a fallen world. It is our choices that cause the evil that exists in the world and not God's direction. As it was in the beginning in the garden, so it is today. But there is good news for those who accept it. This world is temporary, and Jesus Christ is the way to eternal glory forever.

The Bible is clear that God loves us so much that He sent his only begotten Son to die for everyone's sins. And that anyone who calls on his name shall be saved (see John 3:16 and Romans 10:13). The evil that is present today exists solely because of the wickedness of man's heart. Early on in scripture God tells us exactly where man is spiritually. The Bible says, "And GOD saw that the wickedness of man was great in the earth, and that every imagination of the thoughts of his heart was only evil continually" (Genesis 6:5). But God gives us the way out from our sinful nature and the way to reconciliation to God the Father. The Father sent God the Son into the world and died for our sins so that anyone can be saved by God's grace through faith in Jesus Christ.

Anyone who truly believes and confesses that Jesus is the Son of God, born of a virgin, who lived a sinless and perfect life, died on the cross for our sins, physically resurrected after three days, and ascended into heaven and sits at the right hand of God the Father and makes intercession for believers, is born-again and has everlasting life. If you believe that, you have a home that is prepared just for you in glory-land. If you do not believe that and have rejected the gospel and the free gift of salvation, then you have a place reserved for you in the Lake of Fire after the Judgement. God does not want you to face the second death. God does not want you to be eternally condemned because of your sinful nature. He has given you the only way to escape that, and that is through the blood of God the Son, Jesus Christ. The Father loves you and I so much that He sent His Son (God in the flesh) to die in our place. And he continues to plead with us on a daily basis to get our attention so that we will all accept this free gift that man cannot earn on his own.

The Lord pleaded with his chosen people, the Israelites, to repent when he said, "Come now, and let us reason together, saith the LORD: though your sins be as scarlet, they shall be as white as snow; though they be red like crimson, they shall be as wool. If ye be willing and obedient, ye shall eat the good of the land: But if ye refuse and rebel, ye shall be devoured with the sword: for the mouth of the LORD hath spoken it" (Isaiah 1:18-20). Today the Lord is saying the same thing; Come let us reason together. Call on the name of Jesus and be saved. Repent from wickedness, confess Jesus is Lord and believe in your heart and escape the wrath to come. Believe not, and you are condemned already. But it is not because God condones evil, it is because you do.

- **Read Proverbs 6:16-19, Genesis 6:5, Isaiah 1:18-20 & 2 Peter 3:9**
- How does knowing that it is not God's will for any to die and go to hell, change your approach to evangelism?
  - o Do you willingly and openly share the Gosep with others?
  - o How do you answer someone who says God is not a loving father since there is evil in the world?
- Actively practice this week answering the heard questions that you may be faced with.
  - o Get in front of a mirror as if you were answering that question.
  - o Have the scriptures marked in your Bible and ready to go, such as Genesis 6:5 and 2 Peter 3:9 and even search the scriptures for more detailed information regarding the evil that exists in our world today.
- Pray that God would use you to lead people to Christ in Truth and away from the negative lies that are often programmed into the unbeliever's heads.
- Do you know of anyone who may not believe based on their opinion that God cannot be a loving father because of the evil in the world?
- Journal any experiences that you may have had with people who reject Christ because of the evil in the world. Has God used you to impact their life?

THE LORD IS MY SHEPHERD

Many people know the twenty third psalm and can recite it by heart. There are many more people who are at least familiar with the text and can paraphrase it or stumble through it from memory. Even people who are not Christians can tell you they have heard it before and know that it is in the Holy Bible. But few examine the scripture to truly know what that entails. What exactly does it mean to have the Lord as your shepherd? Each line throughout the six verses should resonate with the believer in Christ Jesus. Every word of it should instill a sense of security for the redeemed. Verse one says, "The Lord is my shepherd; I shall not want". Isaiah says this of God, "He shall feed his flock like a shepherd: he shall gather the lambs with his arm, and carry them in his bosom, and shall gently lead those that are with young" (Isaiah 41:11).

A shepherd is loving and ensures that the flock is taken care of and will at all costs defend his sheep. Once you are in his fold, the shepherd looks after you just like all the others. Ezekiel by the Word of God, prophesying about Jesus said, "And I will set up one shepherd over them, and he shall feed them, even my servant David; he shall feed them, and he shall be their shepherd" (Ezekiel 34:23). And Jesus Christ himself said, "I am the good shepherd: the good shepherd giveth his life for his sheep" (John 10:11). What a blessing to know that God the Father, sent God the Son into the world to be our good shepherd. The one who laid down his earthly life for all who call upon his name.

Knowing Jesus Christ as your Lord and Savior puts you in his fold. We are now looked after by the One True God and have our shepherd, Jesus, looking after us. He makes us lie down in green pastures; he leads us beside the still waters. It is Jesus that restores our soul and leads us in the paths of righteousness for his name's sake (See Psalm 23:2-3). Even with storms raging all around us in the life that we now live, we have Jesus watching over us. We have the Holy spirit indwelling in us. The

Shepherd cannot and will not let one of his go. Jesus said. "How think ye? if a man have an hundred sheep, and one of them be gone astray, doth he not leave the ninety and nine, and goeth into the mountains, and seeketh that which is gone astray" (Matthew 18:12)? Immediately prior to this verse Jesus said, "For the Son of man is come to save that which was lost" (Matthew 18:11).

God the father sent God the Son, Jesus Christ, into the world to save those who were lost. And once you have repented and confessed Jesus as Lord and Savior, and believe in your heart, you are in the fold. He will not lose you. You cannot be lost. Even though things around us look bad and things seem to be getting worse, just remember you are in the sheepfold of the Lord Jesus. You have a heavenly home that will not perish. You have eternal life because of the good shepherd. Nothing down here can jeopardize that. Jesus also told us this; "My sheep hear my voice, and I know them, and they follow me: And I give unto them eternal life; and they shall never perish, neither shall any man pluck them out of my hand. My Father, which gave them me, is greater than all; and no man is able to pluck them out of my Father's hand" (John 10:27-29). Once you are in the fold, you are in the fold. How do I know? Because Jesus says so!

We may walk through the valleys of the shadow of death in this life, but we are just passing through. Jesus is walking with us and will see us to the other side. Whom or what shall we fear? Do circumstances dictate whether we belong to Christ? Absolutely not! He prepares a table for us in the presence of our enemies. He anoints us with oil and our cup surely runeth over. Goodness and mercy will follow us all the days of our lives and we will dwell in the house of the Lord forever (see Psalm 23:4-6). I cannot speak for you, the reader, because I do not know your heart. But I can speak for those who are truly born-again believers in Christ. The Lord is my shepherd, and I shall not want. It is my Lord Jesus that saves, protects, guides, builds, prepares, and is coming again. The Lord Jesus is my shepherd. Who is your shepherd?

- **Read Psalm 23, John Chapter 10, Isaiah 41:11, Ezekiel 34:23, Matthew 18:11-12**
- How does knowing Jesus as our Shepherd make you feel?

- Do you feel protected even in times of trouble?
- Do you hear his soft, still voice through the noise of this life telling you it is going to be ok?
- This week keep your eyes steadfastly on Christ and when faced with turmoil, go to the Lord in prayer as always.
- Share your faith with others that may be going through hardships and pray with them.
- Jesus has prepared you for His service and has placed you where you need to be for Him.
- Write in your journal this week how knowing the Good Shepherd is constantly overseeing you within the flock makes you feel. Thank God and praise Him for His provisions. He never fails to sustain us and care for us!

TURN TO GOD & HE WILL TURN TO YOU

I have read stories about people walking away from a helping hand because they were too prideful to accept the help that was offered. Many times, this has led to destruction for the one walking away. I have personally seen this in my life, and if I am to be completely honest, I have even been the one to shun the help of someone. Much like the others, I thought I can do it on my own, or perhaps I can do it better by myself without someone else getting in the way of how I want to do things. While there is nothing wrong with being self-sufficient to an extent, there is something wrong with being so full of pride that you block the blessings of others that God has placed in your path. I have learned this the hard way in my life, but I am so thankful that Jesus is longsuffering towards us, and his mercy and grace is everlasting to those who call upon his name. Sadly, too few have accepted the help that God Almighty has provided to humanity through the atoning blood of Jesus Christ.

The God of all creation loves us so much that he had a plan all along to provide the only way for us to be reconciled back to the Father. He knew we were sinful by nature and that our hearts are continually evil (see Genesis 6:5). But because of His great love towards us, God the Father sent God the Son to die on a cross at Calvary's hill to be the substitute for our sin. Blood is the only acceptable price for the penalty of sin. God Jehovah required the blood of a lamb without blemish from the Hebrews every year for the penalty of their sins. Each year the Jewish people would bring their sin offering to be offered on the altar of the Lord so that their sins would be forgiven for that year. But when God the Father sent God the Son into the world, He sent the only acceptable redemption for all of humanity's sins.

Jesus Christ is the Lamb of God, the one who takes away the sins of the world (see John 1:29). It is by Jesus, the lamb without blemish, and the offering of His blood and the sacrifice of His earthly life, that we are forgiven. Of course, that is only for all who believe. Those who do not are condemned forever (see John 3:18). My question for any and everyone who reads this who is not already saved is, why would you allow your sinful pride to stand in the way of your eternal salvation? God himself has extended the olive leaf of peace unto humanity and asks us to accept it without doing anything for it. All we have to do is believe in our heart, confess with our mouth, and do so with sincere repentance.

Jesus has done all the work for us. There is no other requirement. There is no other payment. There is no other work that can reconcile you and I to God the Father but by Jesus. Jesus himself tells us in the Bible, "...I am the way, the truth, and the life: no man cometh unto the Father, but by me" (John 14:6). There is nothing else anyone can do to get into heaven after this life on earth. Just as Jesus told Nicodemus, I am telling you, you must be born again (see John 3:1-7). This is a free gift. This is the helping hand of God the Father through God the Son. Yet, the mercy and grace of God is walked away from without any regard to the consequences of people's actions simply by foolish and sinful pride. Sadly, the majority of people would rather die and go to hell and face an eternity in the Lake of Fire after the judgement, then turn to Jesus and live for Him. They would rather continue to live the sinful life they are currently because they do not want to give up their "fun." I do not know what you think, but let me tell you hell isn't any fun, and the torment is forever.

Many of the people who have thus far rejected Christ experience extreme highs and lows in life without the true joy that only comes from knowing the Lord. When they are on top, they are exceedingly happy, but when the mountain crumbles they are excruciatingly sorrowful with no hope. Christians have an eternal hope that never fades regardless of circumstances. The Apostle Paul explains it like this, "I can do all things through Christ which strengtheneth me" (Philippians 4:13). If you want to experience joy without end regardless of the situation, turn to Jesus. It is the only way. Just as God told the

Jewish people through the prophet Zechariah, he is telling us today "...
Turn ye unto me, saith the LORD of hosts, and I will turn unto you,
saith the LORD of hosts." (Zechariah 1:3b).

- **Read Zechariah 1:3, John 1:29, 3:1-7, 16-18, 14:6, Philippians 4 (the entire chapter for context purposes)**
- I assume since you are on week Thirty-three that you have placed your faith and trust in Jesus. At least I pray you have.
- As a born-again believer, do you know anyone who is rejecting the Salvation by the Grace of God through faith in Jesus?
- Have they given you a reason?
- Pray for those people this week that God would give them a heart of flesh and remove the scales from heir eyes to see the Truth and respond favorably. Pray that God would use you and other Christians to help lead them to the Truth in righteousness for salvation.
- Journal your interactions with those around you who are non-believers.
- How would you compare their life with those you know who are believers?
- Do they live with hope and if so, what hope do they have?
- Make sure you praise God today and every day for the precious gift of salvation He provided through the sacrifice of His only begotten Son, Jesus.

THE ANCIENT OF DAYS

Everywhere you turn, you can see the devil at work these days, and many are being devoured by his schemes. What is sad, is that many of his minions do not even realize that they are doing his bidding. Here in America, we have cities literally being destroyed by our own citizens in the name of justice. Ironically, the dragon has these people believing that looting, destroying, injuring, and killing is the answer to injustices in the country. Evil being repaid for perceived evil is still evil, no matter how we look at it or how we try to justify it. Evil is evil! The Bible tells us, "Recompense to no man evil for evil. Provide things honest in the sight of all men" (Romans 12:7). However, many people committing these very sins are doing so while touting their belief in Jesus. These false Christians are only deceiving themselves.

The Bible says, "Be not deceived; God is not mocked: for whatsoever a man soweth, that shall he also reap" (Galatians 6:7). These people are ignorantly destroying themselves in the process of committing their atrocities. God will recompense your evil ways upon you, regardless of what you say you believe. If you are a follower of Jesus Christ then you must be a follower of His Word, for He is the Word of God (see John1:1-3). The Bible gives us our directions for life, yet many of the so-called Christians today ignore His Word and give way to their deceitful lusts of the heart. This evil that is tormenting our nation at the moment can cause any normal person to be distraught and filled with anxiety out of concern for our republic. But be of good cheer, this too shall pass, and it will not stand.

As a Bible-believing, born-again Christian, saved by the grace of God through faith in Jesus Christ and by the power of the Holy Spirit, we have the promises granted unto us in God's own Word. The true Christian knows that the devil's reign of terror is only temporary and that one day it will all end abruptly, and he too will face the judgement that is reserved for him and his followers. Who are Satan's followers you ask? Anyone who is not a Christian. Anyone who denies Christ is a follower of the deceiver. You are either saved by grace or you are not. You are either born-again or you are not. You are either with and for Jesus or you are against Him. There is no middle ground. There is no fence to straddle.

By not choosing to follow Jesus, people have made a choice to go the way of the devil. Jesus says, "He that is not with me is against me; and he that gathereth not with me scattereth abroad" (Matthew 12:30). Those of us who are with Him, know without a doubt, that the Lord himself will call us home to be with him forever (see 1 Thessalonians 4:13-18). What a glorious day that will be for Christians everywhere. For we shall forever be with the Lord in a new body, no more to suffer the slings and arrows of this life, and we will be basking in the glory of the Lord! But for those who remain on earth, woe unto them! As much as a comfort the Word of God is to the believer, it is disturbing to the lost soul. They will receive the same fate as the one which they follow during their earthly life. As much as the believer looks forward to the day we are caught up with the Lord in the air, the unsaved sinner dreads it in their soul. Even those who deny the Word of God and His power know in their heart that the day is coming and will soon be upon them.

The Prophet Daniel wrote about the revelation of the judgement long before the revelation was given to the Apostle John on the isle of Patmos. To those who think the evil today will last forever, to those who think rebellion is the answer and that their actions will not be met with righteous judgement, God presents you the truth. Daniel writes, "I beheld till the thrones were cast down and the Ancient of days did sit, whose garment was white as snow, and the hair of his head like the pure wool: his throne was like the fiery flame, and his wheels as burning fire" (Daniel 7:9). He goes on to tell us, "…the judgment was set, and the books were opened" (Daniel 7:10b). The believer is comforted by these very words, for we know we are not appointed unto God's wrath (see 1 Thessalonians 5:9). However, the unbeliever should be terrified. There is a judgment coming whether you believe it or not and the Ancient of days will recompense your ways upon you and it will be an eternal sentence.

- **Read Romans 12:7, Galatians 6:7, John 1:1-3, Matthew 12:30, 1 Thessalonians 4:13-18, Daniel 7:9-10 and 1 Thessalonians 5:9**
- Does knowing that Christ will return to call believers home give you confidence and excitement, or do you fear and worry?
- How does knowing the Bible speaks of the coming Judgement shape how you live your life before others?
- As a Christian take comfort in knowing you are saved and not reserved for the Warth of God. But at the same time, let this knowledge motivate you to tell others of the saving Garce of God through faith in Jesus.
  - Without that salvation people will face the coming judgement.
- Pray that God will lead your lost loved ones and friends to faith in Jesus. Pray for all the lost souls while you are at it.
- Give God praise and thanksgiving for revealing His truth to you and saving your soul from the coming judgment.
- Journal this week how God is using you and other believers around you to share the Gospel with others.

HAVE NO FELLOWSHIP
WITH DARKNESS

Not everything is as it appears to be. This goes for churches as well. Just because there is a steeple outside and a pulpit, pews, hymnals, pianos, and organs on the inside does not make it a Bible believing church. There are in fact too few Bible believing fundamental churches today that preach sound biblical doctrine. The big craze of the day is to have a modern worship service with rock bands that play contemporary Christian music (CCM) in place of doctrinally sound hymns. The music is played more to edify oneself than it is to give honor, praise and glory to our Lord and Savior Jesus Christ.

In fact, when I mention this to people today, I get a response of, "but these songs make us feel so much better." If what you do in worship is about you feeling better, then you are worshipping the wrong person. That is not to say that you should not feel good about going to church and worshipping the Lord, because you should. But your motivation behind worship should be to bring honor, praise, and glory to the Lord, not to yourself. That is actually what our motivation should be in every act that we do on a daily basis, not just on Sundays. Now I know we all come short of the glory of God, but we should not deliberately come short of His glory.

One extremely popular CCM song is a song called "Oceans" by a group called Hillsong United. These lyrics are generically written and can be applied to just about anyone or any faith that you apply it to. Never once is the name of the Lord mentioned, praised, or honored. Who calls you out? Whose grace abounds? What spirit leads you? And whose name do you call upon? Oh, but how the song makes us "feel" good! Furthermore, the group Hillsong United is from the Hillsong church, which is a modern church with pagan practices and eastern mysticism intermingled with Christian faith. New York Hillsong church pastor Carl Lentz is on video stating he does not believe Jesus is the only way to heaven (I Think Biblically, n.d.). This can easily be viewed on YouTube from his appearances on several talk shows, to include Orpah Winfrey's. Yet the modern churches of today celebrate this movement and the music that is brought about by it.

Modernism and Neo-Evangelism spawned from a movement in the 20th century that saw a move away from fundamental doctrine to a liberal, easier on the ears teaching. They have abandoned fundamental doctrines that are the backbone and necessities of the Christian faith such as, the Virgin Birth, the Deity of Jesus Christ, the blood atonement, and the Holy Bible as the divinely inspired, infallible and inerrant and sufficient Word of God. They have replaced these with a free-for-all, feel good gospel that is no gospel at all. They tickle the ears of the hearer in an attempt to make them feel good about themselves regardless of their sins and need for repentance, and salvation that can only be given by the grace of God through faith in Jesus Christ. They have quit preaching the Truth of the Bible and are now teaching a universal acceptance religion.

These so-called churches are more worried about inclusion and acceptance of all people regardless of beliefs and sin because we now live in a society where "everybody gets a trophy." Well, let me be the first to say just in case you did not already know, everybody does not go to heaven just because they want to or just because they think they are good people. Jesus says you must repent or perish (see Luke 13:3). Paul tells us that you must confess and believe on the name of the Lord Jesus in order to be saved (See Romans 10:9-10). Jesus himself tells us in John 14:6 that he is "The Way, The Truth and The Life" and that "No man cometh to the Father but by Me."

So how is it that so many can be fooled into believing the lie that is being presented in our churches today? We have left Truth behind in favor of a feel-good message that makes everybody happy regardless of what they do, say, or believe. They say we can all come together and get along and everything will be fine. If you are in a church that teaches and supports this, I implore you to get away from it. Either find another pastor or find another church. Because the Bible is our authority, not man. The Bible says "...let God be true and every man a liar" (Romans

3:4). God tells us to be followers of Him, not the world. So why are we trying so hard to put the world in our churches? The Word of God says, "And have no fellowship with the unfruitful works of darkness, but rather reprove them" (Ephesians 5:11). As your brother in Christ and in truth and love, I beg you to stand firm on the Word and be not unequally yoked. As followers of Jesus, we should have no fellowship with the darkness.

- **Read Luke 13:3, Romans 3:4, 10:9-10 &13, Ephesians 5:11**
- According to the Bible, is Christ "a" way or is He "The Way"?
- How does knowing that there are major Churches spreading false teachings affect you as a Christian?
- Does it make you want to spread the Truth more?
- How do you think supporting music from artists that come out of that false teaching churches affect the message that is being spread throughout the world today?
- Pray that God would reveal the false teachers and expose them for who they are, and that people will turn from them. I also encourage you to stick with the old doctrinally sound hymns rather than lean on the modern contemporary Christian music that is financially supporting these false teachers.
- Use your journal to express how this week's devotional made you feel.
- Did it upset you or did it solidify what you already knew?
- Do you think the music you listen to matters when it comes to being a Christian?
- Why or why not?

GATHER OR SCATTER

During the earthly ministry of Jesus, there was a particular day when some questioned whether or not Jesus was the Messiah or if he was actually of the chief of the devils. In Luke chapter 11, Jesus had cast out a devil from a man who had previously been unable to speak but began to speak after this miracle Jesus performed. Some bystanders said that Jesus was casting out the devils through Beelzebub. But then Jesus sets the record straight by asking them a simple question; by whom do your sons cast out devils? This comes after the famous passage that Abraham Lincoln quoted 150 years ago concerning the civil war strife in America. "But he, knowing their thoughts, said unto them, every kingdom divided against itself is brought to desolation; a house divided against a house falleth" (Luke 11:17). He is asking them how could an agent of Beelzebub be working against Beelzebub? The answer is obvious; he could not, and he would not work against himself. Likewise, neither does God.

Jesus is the Son of God, who is God in the flesh. Since before the foundations of the earth were laid Jesus has done the work of God the Father. Jesus was working to bring glory to our heavenly Father by casting out demons in Luke chapter 11, and He continues to do so today for anyone who willingly seeks him, repents, confesses, and believes in their heart that Jesus Christ is their Lord and Savior. There is no respect of persons with God (see Acts 10:34-35). All who come to Jesus are accepted if they repent, confess, and believe. And there is the heart of the matter. Saying something is one thing. It all boils down to what you honestly believe.

There are many that say they believe in Jesus but outwardly show worldly desires rather than center their life on doing the things that are pleasing unto the Lord. It is true that we are not saved by works. The Apostle Paul says, "For by grace are ye saved through faith; and that not of yourselves: it is the gift of God: Not of works, lest any man should boast" (Ephesians 2:8-9). However, a saved person seeks to live a life that is pleasing to the Lord, not work against Him. Some people may not realize that they are working against the Lord by merely living the same life they always have. But the Lord tells us that we are working against Him if we do not live according to His directions for our lives. Jesus says, "He that is not with me is against me; and he that gathereth not with me scattereth" (Luke 11:23).

If you are not working in some fashion to gather then you are by Jesus' definition, scattering. The Bible says, "For we are his workmanship, created in Christ Jesus unto good works, which God hath before ordained that we should walk in them" (Ephesians 2:10). God has ordained that the saved person do good works and walk accordingly. We should not continue to walk according to our lustful flesh. If I were getting ready to go to a wedding ceremony and took a shower, got all dressed in my finest clothes, I would not go roll around with the pigs. But that is what many have done today. They know they are sinners and need Christ for salvation, so they confess with their mouths and say they believe in their hearts, then turn around and go back to what it was that Jesus saved them from in the first place. Too often there is no evidence of a changed life only brought about by the indwelling Holy Spirit.

As we come to the Lord sorrowfully, knowing we are all sinners and need Christ for our salvation, let us do so with a repenting heart. To repent means to turn from. We are asking for forgiveness of our sins, so let us turn from the sins we know we need saving from. We cannot do this alone, which is why we must be sincere when we ask for forgiveness and call upon our Lord Jesus to save us. If you honestly believe in your heart Jesus is your Lord and Savior, ask Him to change your life. You and I cannot do it on our own strength. We will fail every time doing it alone. Jesus told His disciples, "And whatsoever ye shall ask in my name, that will I do, that the Father may be glorified in the Son" (John 14:13). Seek to please Him, not yourselves, and He will perform it through you. But remember we are either for Him or against Him, there is no middle ground. We are either gatherers together with Christ or we simply continue to scatter abroad.

- **Read all of Luke Chapter 11, Acts 10:34-35, John 14:13 and Ephesians 2:8-10.**
- Are you a gatherer or a scatterer?
- Are you allowing the Lord to work through you or are you complacent in the faith?
- How has God used you to spread the seeds of the Gospel message?
- Have you ever resisted doing what the Holy Spirit has led you to do?
- Pray that the Lord will provide you with the strength, and courage to perform His good works through you and share the Gospel of Jesus with those around you.
- Don't get discouraged, God is with you, and I am praying for you as well.
- Don't forget to keep journaling how God is working in your life and write down the experiences you have had.
- Can you see your own spiritual growth?

THE TWO SISTERS

In the book of Ezekiel God speaks through the prophet and tells the story of two sisters who played the harlot that cost them more than they bargained for. In Ezekiel 23, God says that Aholah and Aholibah committed whoredoms with their neighbors. But God does not leave us in the dark about who these two sisters actually are. He says that Aholah is Samaria and Aholibah is Jerusalem. He then explains that the whoredoms they committed were the acts of seeking after the lifestyle, culture, and riches of neighboring nations. Aholah doted on Assyria and Aholibah doted on both the Assyrians and the Chaldeans. They turned their back on living the way God instructed them to live, and they did so even after knowing that God had delivered them out of Egypt into the Land of Milk and Honey.

God called the Hebrew people His people and the apple of his eye as he continued to bless them because of the Abrahamic covenant. The Hebrew people had been one nation, but over the course of time they became a divided nation. The northern kingdom of Israel consisted of ten tribes and the southern kingdom of Judah consisted of two tribes. The northern kingdom's capitol city was Samaria, whereas Judah's capitol city was Jerusalem. Thus, we see God telling His own chosen people that they had committed whoredoms by seeking after the glitz and glamour of the neighboring nations. Rather than living in accordance with the statues God had given them through Moses and living contently with all that God had blessed them with, they chose to seek things unholy. Furthermore, that is how they came to have kings to begin with; they wanted to be like other nations.

Jesus said, "Every kingdom divided against itself is brought to desolation; and every city or house divided against itself shall not stand:" (Matthew 12:25). That held true in the Old Testament, it held true in the days that Jesus walked in the flesh on earth, and it still holds true today. Seeking after things of this world is called covetousness and idolatry and it leads to destruction. The nation of Israel and of Judah both were brought low because of their whoredoms. Israel was overtaken by the Assyrians and Judah overtaken by the Chaldeans. The divided kingdoms of God's people were taken into captivity by the very same people they admired and sought to be like. Furthermore, it was ordained by God Almighty Himself. The Bible says, "Therefore thus saith the Lord GOD; Because thou hast forgotten me, and cast me behind thy back, therefore bear thou also thy lewdness and thy whoredoms." (Ezekiel 23:35). Then God explains why he causes this to occur. "And they shall recompense your lewdness upon you, and ye shall bear the sins of your idols: and ye shall know that I am the Lord GOD: (Ezekiel 23:49).

I hope and pray that whoever is reading this right now can see the parallels between the Hebrew people in Ezekiel's time and the American Christian today. The Church in America has gone the way of ancient Samaria and Jerusalem. We have left our first love and gone after the riches and cultures of others and have intermingled faiths. We have been enticed by worldly things and have allowed worldly things to infiltrate our churches. Many of our churches today look no different than a nightclub or coffee shop. There is seemingly no difference between the church and the world, and it appears to be drifting further and further from Truth. The image is becoming so blurred that the Christian today cannot tell the difference let alone someone who is seeking the truth. And just as God told Ezekiel to "declare unto them their abominations" (Ezekiel 23:36b) pastors, preachers, evangelists, and teachers need to be declaring the abominations today.

God is a God of love, grace, and mercy. He loves us so much that He sent Jesus into this world to be the payment for our sins. The Lord Jesus willingly laid down His life on the cross at Calvary so that we might have eternal life by faith in believing in the Son of God. And God has called all believers to be holy as he is holy. The Apostle Peter reminds us by writing, "Wherefore gird up the loins of your mind, be sober, and hope to the end for the grace that is to be brought unto you at the revelation of Jesus Christ; As obedient children, not fashioning yourselves according to the former lusts in your ignorance:

But as he which hath called you is holy, so be ye holy in all manner of conversation; Because it is written, Be ye holy; for I am holy" (1 Peter 1:13-16).

So, today I encourage all believers in Christ Jesus to walk with Him in accordance with His Holy Word in the Bible. Knowing that we all sin and come short of the glory of God as explained in Romans 3:23, we still should not surrender to the flesh. We should strive to be holy in all manner of conversation and deed. I pray that we learn from the two sisters and forsake the world and all its treasures. Let us return to our first love in Christ Jesus and help each other in our godly walk daily.

- **Read Ezekiel 23, Matthew 12:25 & 1 Peter 1:13-16**
- Spend time this week contemplating the historical story in Ezekiel 23.
- Do you see the parallels between ancient Israel and us today?
- How do you think you can make a difference as an individual?
- Start each day brand new, even if you messed up yesterday. Wake up and tell the Lord you are His and want to do His will.
- Pray that God will fill you with His Holy Spirit and guide you in all righteousness and lead you where He wants you to be and to say what he wants you to say.
- Record your observations in your journal of the worldliness around us, and how your life is different because of Christ.

MANNA FOR THE SOUL

In Exodus we see the account of the Hebrew people walking in the wilderness. God used Moses to lead his people out of Egypt after four hundred years of captivity. In chapter sixteen the people become famished and begin to grumble amongst themselves and eventually their murmurings were directed at Moses and at God. The very same God that freed His chosen people by miraculous signs and wonders. The same God that parted the Red Sea so that they might cross on dry ground and avoid sure death at the hands of Pharaoh and his army. At this point in the story, it appears that none of that mattered anymore to the Hebrew people. They were hungry and unhappy. They even suggest that it would have been better for them to have remained in captivity and died at the hands of Pharaoh rather than to be set free from bondage. I do not know about you, but I think that is a sad state of affairs. But because the Lord is righteous and merciful He provides. God rains down Manna from heaven to feed the Hebrews in the wilderness.

God Almighty provided for his people in the wilderness and not one person lacked the bread that he or she needed to sustain themselves. Once again, God performed another miraculous event that helped the Hebrew people survive during a desperate time. God continues to provide Manna from heaven today for everyone that receives it. In our most desperate situations that we have ever been in, are currently going through, or may go through in the future, God has provided the bread we all need to sustain each of us. But just like the days of the Hebrews wondering in the wilderness, we must collect what God has provided for us. God does not force feed us anything. He provides sustenance for us, but it is up to us to pick it up and consume it for our good. God gives each of us free will to make those choices on our own. But unfortunately, many people leave the Manna where it sits and never consume it so that we may be filled.

In Matthew chapter four our Lord Jesus is in the wilderness for forty days and forty nights where he has fasted and is suffering from his own hunger. Remember that Jesus is both fully man and fully God. While on earth in the flesh He experienced what we all experience, but without sin. It was at this point that Satan saw Jesus at His most vulnerable state and began to tempt Him. The Bible says that the "tempter came to him and said if thou art the Son of God, command that these stones be made bread" (Matthew 4:3). But Jesus withstood the devil's temptation, even though he was hungered just as any man would be. Rather than give into temptation, Jesus responded to Satan and said, "it is written, man shall not live by bread alone, but by every word that proceedeth out of the mouth of God" (Matthew 4:4). Jesus was referring to Moses words in Deuteronomy 8:3, where Moses is warning against forgetting God's mercies on His people.

Sadly, today I believe many of the Lord's children have forgotten who supplies our every need. We have been so tempted by the world and all it has to offer that we have simply quit eating the most important nourishment there is. The prince of this world, Satan, has disguised himself and the world as our friend and is leading more people astray each day. Unwittingly people are being led to hell, the whole while believing they are ok. This is why it is so important that everyone reads the Bible for themselves. The Manna from heaven is sitting there waiting for you to pick it up, consume it, chew on it, and digest it. Do not believe something because I said it, a pastor or preacher said it, or a television evangelist said it. Be like the Berean people in the book of Acts chapter. Believe it because you read and studied it for yourself.

The Word of God provides everything you need and all the answers you are searching for in this world. "For the word of God is quick, and powerful, and sharper than any two-edged sword, piercing even to the dividing asunder of soul and spirit, and of the joints and marrow, and is a discerner of the thoughts and intents of the heart" (Hebrews 4:12). God loves us so much that He has never left us. He is right there waiting for each of us to pick up His Word and learn from Him directly. He has provided the bread we all need, His Word! Will you gather it up and consume it today? It is Manna for the soul!

- **Read Exodus 16, Matthew 4:1-11, Deuteronomy 8:3 & Hebrews 4:12**
- You have The Word of God right in front of you to consume every day.
- Are you feasting on the manna, or are you allowing the birds to pluck it up?
- You have made it to week thirty-eight of this weekly devotional, so I assume you are sticking with it.
- I encourage you to read your Bible daily and allow God to instruct you in righteousness with His Holy Word and be led by Holy Ghost in all wisdom and understanding.
- Don't neglect time with God, He has never neglected us.
- Pray for God to continue to reveal to you His Truths in His Word and ask Him to help you apply them to your life each and every day, walking gently with the Lord Jesus.
- Write down in your journal how spending time with God in His Word has changed your life and give God the glory for what He is doing for you!

THE AUTHOR AND FINISHER

As the years go by it is growing increasingly clearer that more people are turning away from the truth. As a preacher of the Gospel of Jesus Christ I often find myself in discussions with non-believers. I have personally heard numerous reasons why people say they do not believe in the saving grace of God through the precious atoning blood of Jesus. However, I must say that the non-believer is easier to speak with than the believer who has not grown in their relationship with Christ. I can explain the Gospel (the death, burial, and resurrection) of Jesus to someone outside of Christianity and have them understand it plainly. Whether they choose to accept the free gift of eternal life in heaven is up to them. But at least I know they understood the message and get the importance of why God sent His only begotten Son to die for us. They understand that our salvation cannot be earned by anything we do on earth. They realize, as the prophet Isaiah penned, "But we are all as an unclean thing, and all our righteousnesses are as filthy rags;" (Isaiah 64:6a). They comprehend the necessity of our heavenly Father being the only one who could provide the prefect sacrifice by which we could be reconciled to Him.

While the Gospel is easy to understand, there are many "Christians" who cannot plainly grasp the importance of growing their relationship with Christ. Many of the professing Christians today simply have not understood that Christianity is a "relationship" and not a "religion." A follower of Christ is not one in word only, but indeed and truth. But there lies the issue that the church is faced with today. As a believer in Christ, you become part of the "Body of Christ" which is the church. However, the church today does not realize that we are to grow in Christ daily and turn (repent) from the wickedness of the world. I am willing to say that many I talk with today that call themselves Christians are the first to dispute with their brethren over a scriptural truth. The reason is because they do not know scripture. They merely rely on the pastor to tell them what they need to know, and if the pastor does not say it, then it must not be. This is ludicrous.

A person cannot have a relationship with another without getting to know one another. We cannot build a foundational bond unless we get to the foundation of all things. If you attend church one Sunday a week, every Sunday for a year, you will have gone to Church fifty-two times and might receive twenty-six hours of preaching. There are sixty-six books, eleven hundred and eighty-nine chapters, and over thirty-one thousand verses in the King James Bible. All of which is the Word of God given to us by divine inspiration and God breathed. There is no way to get the full measure of what God is revealing to us, by simply hearing and reading along on Sunday morning. Furthermore, the Word of God is "living." He has provided a message to all of us as a whole, and to each of us individually. We should be spending time nurturing our relationship as we grow in fellowship with Christ. The only way to do so is through prayer and daily reading of the scripture. Not reading just to read and check the block but reading so that we may know Him better. Then we should put what we read into effect.

When I explain this to others who profess Christianity, I am often hit with "the Bible was written by men" or "the Bible is flawed" or something along those lines. This tells me a lot about who I am talking to when I encounter such absurdity. If you do not believe in the divinely inspired, infallible, inerrant, and sufficient Word of God then you yourself are at odds with the Truth. John chapter one tells us that Jesus is the Word. God tells us that He has preserved His Word (see Psalm 12:6-7), and the Bible itself is the authority for all Christians. Authority can only come from the Author. All Christians should be, "Looking unto Jesus the author and finisher of our faith; who for the joy that was set before him endured the cross, despising the shame, and is set down at the right hand of the throne of God" (Hebrews 12:2). Unfortunately, today there are many who are Christians in name only. They do not walk in truth because they do not understand the truth. They do not understand the truth because they truly do not know the Author.

- **Read Isaiah 64:6, John 1:1-3, Psalms 12:6-7 & Hebrews 12:2**
- How well do you know God?
- In order to have a relationship you must spend time with someone. So, how much time are spending with God in prayer and study of His Word?
- How has your time alone with God's Word helped you in your relationship with Him?
    - o Have you begun searching for things on your own through His Word?
- As you continue to grow in your relationship by spending more time in the Bible and in prayer, I encourage you to apply His Word in your everyday life and let others see Him in you.
- Ask God in prayer to help others see Him in you and to allow you to be a better witness for Him.
- Journal your thoughts on how well you believe you know God through His Word and by spending alone time in prayer with Him.

LIBERTY THROUGH CHRIST

There is a lot of talk on social media these days about the loss of freedoms. While it is true that many of the freedoms, we enjoyed in yesteryear have vanished, Christians have a hope that surpasses any resemblance of manmade independence. People aren't free because they pay less taxes. People are not free because they can choose their own insurance. People are not free just because they have independent choices to make free from retribution by the government. Although those are great ideals of a free society, those things do not really declare your personal independence in this world. However, it is becoming more evident that the things of this world are what we hold to the highest esteem.

As a veteran of the armed forces of this nation, I hold freedoms near and dear to my heart. I served to protect the freedoms that our forefathers fought to earn and preserve. Some veterans have lost their physical independence due to injuries and others lost their lives. We as Americans should continue to do all we can to help protect our civil liberties in this great union. That means we should vote in a manner that will preserve our sovereignty, not our purse. As we celebrate Veteran's Day and Memorial Day each year, let us never forget the sacrifices that were made in order for us to enjoy the freedoms that we still hold on to in this country.

As a Christian there is one thing and one thing only that makes me free. It is the sacrifice made by our Lord and Savior Jesus Christ on the cross at Calvary. We have a God that loves us so much that He sent His only begotten Son into the world to be the only sacrifice worthy enough to pay our sin debt. As a born-again believer in Christ, we have been set free from the bondage of sin. Because we have been set free from sin, we should never again return to that which held us in bondage. The Apostle Paul says it best, "Stand fast therefore in the liberty wherewith Christ hath made us free and be not entangled again with the yoke of bondage" (Galatians 5:1). Nevertheless, that is what many professing Christians have done.

Just as we complain about the freedoms that have been taken from us in our country, it seems as though that Christian liberty has been snatched from us as well. But that really is not the case at all. Our American freedoms have slowly been given away, not taken. They have been given away by people seeking their own personal gain rather than preserving our sovereignty as a nation. And much like our American freedoms have deteriorated over the years, so have the professing Christian's liberties. That is because there seems to be little to no difference between the professing Christian and the world. And that is not how God intended it to be. We are called to be Holy; to be sperate from the world. Yet the church looks more like the world every day. The church members are shackling themselves back into the chains of bondage of sin.

If we are to be the example to others in this dark world, we must be the example that God has called us to be and not the example the world tells us to be. Otherwise, we are no example at all. How can we be set free from sin and then welcome sin into our lives? How can we praise God that He has set us free, then turn around and continue to do what He set us free from? The answer is obvious. We cannot. The Apostle Paul says, "For, brethren, ye have been called unto liberty; only use not liberty for an occasion to the flesh, but by love serve one another" (Galatians 5:13). We should not use our freedoms to continue to sin, but rather live the life that Christ commands us to live. Our Liberty frees us from sin, so we should not serve the flesh but serve the Lord. This is the Liberty we have through Jesus Christ. That Liberty can never be taken from you.

- **Read all of Galatians this week (it is only six chapters)**
- Paul called the Galatians foolish because they believed a lie and turned back to the law and were not living by faith alone.
  - o How have you grown in your faith since being saved?
  - o How have you grown in knowledge of His Holy Word?
  - o Are you applying this knowledge in your life?

- o Are you helping other Christians develop their faith walk as well?
- Spend time this week in prayer asking God to reveal to you how you can take the next step of faith in your life, for your own good but also for His Glory.
- Record in your journal how Christ is performing His good work through you, not for vain glory but for His glory and the advancement of the Gospel.

CHRISTIAN OBSERVANCES

The Jewish nation of Israel was commanded to observe certain feasts by God. The seven Jewish Feasts are, Passover, Unleavened Bread, First Fruits, Pentecost, Trumpets, Atonement and Tabernacle. These feasts are more than tradition to Israel. These were indeed commanded observances by Almighty Jehovah. Although it is extremely important for Christians to know the Bible and understand the historical importance of these events, along with the significance of how these feasts point to our Lord and Savior Jesus Christ, these observances are not for us. In fact, if you read, study, and understand the Bible you will find that Christians are not commanded to have any of these sacramental observances. Furthermore, there are only two ordnances that a believer in Christ is to partake in by faith in Jesus: believer's baptism and the Lord's Supper.

Believer's baptism is only done when a person has repented of his or her sins, confessed with their mouth and believe in their heart that Jesus Christ is Lord. A Christening or infant baptism does not in any way, shape, or form save a child from condemnation. Furthermore, a believer's baptism is only an outward show of the inward faith one has put in Jesus Christ and His finished work on the Cross at Calvary (See Matthew 28:19-20 and Romans 6:4). When a Christian is publicly baptized, we are saying that we have been renewed and regenerated by Christ with the indwelling Holy Spirit and showing the world that we are a new creature. The old man is buried in the likeness of Jesus' death by emersion and raised in the likeness of His resurrection. This can only be done when one has reached an age where they are accountable for their own actions and understand the significance of salvation.

The Lord's Supper is symbolic of the Last Supper with the Apostles. The breaking and consumption of unleavened bread is symbolic of the breaking of Jesus' body that He willingly broke for all who receive

Him as Lord and Savior. Drinking wine (grape juice) is symbolic of the blood Jesus willingly shed for the believer in Christ; it is the New Testament in His blood. Jesus told his apostles to observe these things (see Matthew 26:26-29). The Apostle Paul instructs the church to observe the Lord's Supper in the same manner in which Jesus commanded (see 1 Corinthians 11:23-26). This is to only be observed by Christians. Paul warns against the unbeliever partaking in the Lord's Supper but tells us to examine ourselves if we are worthy or not in 1 Corinthians 11: 27 and 28.

These are the only two ordnances in the Bible for the Christian. Nowhere in scripture does the Lord tell us to observe any other; not feasts and celebrations, not the traditions of men, not paganistic rituals and not worldly holidays. That does not mean you cannot assemble together in fellowship and praise Jesus for your salvation at any time. We are commanded to do so in Hebrews 10:25. We are even told what day of the week the church assembles; "And upon the first day of the week, when the disciples came together to break bread, Paul preached unto them, ready to depart on the morrow; and continued his speech until midnight" (Acts 20:7). Thus, we know from Scripture that we assemble on the Lord's Day, the first day of the week, which is Sunday.

Many Christians today are intermingling their faith with worldly and manmade traditions that have nothing to do with Christianity. This is dangerous. The Lord warned the Hebrew people not to intermingle with the world in the Old Testament and they did it anyway, which led to destruction. As Christians we should not bring worldly traditions, and celebrations into our churches or our homes. We are after all the church, the body of Christ. We should focus our attention and energy on Christ and doing what He has asked us to do and what He has commanded us to do. Rather than worry ourselves with the traditions of man, let us observe the Word of God and preach the Gospel of Christ to every creature and make disciples of all nations. Let us assemble on Sundays and receive the Lord's Supper together on occasion and let us baptize in the name of the father, the Son, and the Holy Ghost. Jesus says, "If ye love me, keep my commandments: (John 14:15). Let us keep His commandments not our own.

- **Read Matthew 26:26-29 & 28:19-20, Acts 20:7, Romans 6:4, 1 Corinthians 11:23-28 & Hebrews 10:25**
- Did you previously know that there are only two observances for the Christian mentioned in the New Testament?
- As a born-again believer, have you been publicly baptized professing your faith before everyone?
- Do you partake in the Lord's Super?
- As A Christian do you think it is appropriate to participate in events such as Halloween?
    - How about Jewish events?
- Do you think God wants the Church to intermingle the world in with faith in Jesus?
- Ask God in prayer to show you in His Word the observances we should and should not be involved with.
    - Search the scriptures for yourself to find anything else a Christian should observe.
- Record your thoughts on Christian Observances in your journal.

NOT FOR SHOW

There are a lot of great Christian organizations and many more individual Christians, which go out of their way to be the hands and feet of God. They extend the helping hand to those in need, always seeking to support the church and even those outside of the body of Christ. How blessed we truly are to be used by our Lord and Savior for His glory, honor, and praise! As a born-again believer in Jesus Christ, you have been granted special gifts from the Holy Spirit that are to be used in the edification of the Church, presenting the gospel to others, reproving and correcting each other within the church, and delivering the love of God and the Gospel to all of humanity. How great a blessing it is to be utilized by our Heavenly Father for His good pleasure.

However, there are some that at times have drifted from the purpose and direction of these wonderful gifts. Not that the people have somehow become bad, but they have allowed that old sinful pride, an instrument of the devil, to take root. Understanding that helping others in need and doing good for others makes us feel good, sometimes that feeling becomes the focus point of the reason we are doing what we do altogether. Jesus says, "Take heed that ye do not your alms before men, to be seen of them: otherwise ye have no reward of your Father which is in heaven" (Matthew 6;1). He goes on to tell us not to sound a trumpet every time you do your good deeds. He then compares that action to hypocrisy. We do not and should not be doing anything unto ourselves or for the purpose of glorifying any mere man. That includes me. That includes you. Jesus says that when people do this, they already have their reward.

Nevertheless, many today have fallen for the deception of the devil and have given into the deceitful lusts of the flesh. Humans want to feel good about themselves and so they do feel good about themselves. Rather than doing things because it is just the right thing to do, or because Jesus says to do them, we often go out of our way to let everyone around us know just what we did, and how important it was. But our Lord says, "But when thou doest alms, let not thy left hand know what thy right hand doeth:" (Matthew 6:3). We do not need to let anyone know what we just did for Joe down the street. God already knows what you did, because He was the one who put it on your heart in the first place. God tells us to do it in secret and He will reward you openly. Why would we exchange God's blessing for the reward of a man? That just does not make much sense to a Bible believing Christian. Or at least it should not.

I am not saying to stop doing good for others. I am not saying that at all and neither does the Bible teach that. We are to do good unto others. We are to love one another as Christ loves the Church. We are to love not only our brethren in Christ, but also our enemies and pray for them as well. Jesus wants us all to be His hands and feet. He wants us all to willingly surrender to Him and be used By Him and for Him. It is all for the glory of God, the Father, Son, and Holy Ghost. In fact, that is why we are here on earth. We are here for His glory, honor, and praise, not our own vain glory. So, go out and be the hands and feet of Jesus. Do good and extend the Love of God to everyone. But you do not have to be loud about it. God knows and He will reward you. He chose you and I to do His good will. Let us do His work and give God all the glory in everything we do.

- **Read Matthew 6:1-8 & Matthew 5:43-48**
- Do you know anyone who likes to sound the Alarm over their good deeds?
- How does that make you feel?
- Have you ever been tempted to tell the world about all the good you have done?
  - o If we are honest, we probably all have at one time or another in our life.
  - o Let us lay that aside and put it behind us knowing God's Word.
- Do You help others in need within your community?
  - o What about those who may not even like you?

- Pray that God will lead you to help those in need and provides you the resources to help.
  - o Don't worry if anyone sees you doing it. God sees it!
- Record in your journal how God is using you to help those around you and also how it makes you feel to be useful for God's glory.

BY FAITH

Hebrews tells us, "By faith Enoch was translated that he should not see death; and was not found, because God had translated him: for before his translation he had this testimony, that he pleased God" (Hebrews 11:5). Of course, this is referring to Enoch of the Old Testament who "walked with God: and he was not; for God took him" (Genesis 5:24). As my Pastor the Late Howard Cox once preached, this is a beautiful picture of the rapture of the church. This is a portrait of the greatest event that our future holds for the church of Christ. As a believer in Jesus who has confessed and repented from sin, Christians look forward to the day when Jesus shall pierce the sky and call his bride home forever to be with Him (See 1 Thessalonians 4:13-18).

However, there are many professing Christians today that will not be caught up with the Lord in the air on that day. Nor shall they enter into heaven if they pass from this life before the rapture occurs. The reason is they are professing with their mouth only and are not truly believers in their hearts. Yes, many people today continue to say they are Christian but continue to live a life that is no different than the world in which we live in. Furthermore, there are many professing Christians who strive to act worldly so as to make Christianity cool. This is part of the false gospel that is leading many to ruin and those who are leading the way will pay for their errors. What people need to realize is that you cannot fool anyone but yourself when it comes to being born-again. The evidence of a regenerated life is in the manner in which we now live. No more a slave to sin, we put off the old man and put on the new (see Colossians 3:8-9).

Our church had a guest speaker. A 22-year-old, a self-confessing drug user and dealer, who has been saved by the grace of God through faith in Jesus Christ, has given his life to the Lord and is now an evangelist and preacher of the gospel of Jesus Christ. It is not the words that merely come out of his mouth that indicate the change in his life. The change is evident in how he now lives his life for our Lord and Savior. He is no longer in bondage to the sinful life he once lived. He is now free from sin and on fire for our Lord and his mission is to tell the world how they can become regenerated themselves. Just as this young man put it that day from the pulpit, every true preacher has preached it, and the Bible tells us, that the change is not in and of ourselves. It is Christ who lives in us by the power of the indwelling Holy Spirit that makes the change in our lives.

When someone truly comes to the Lord with repentance, they are broken. We know that we are dirty, filthy sinners that are truly deserving death (See Romans 3:23). We know that there is only one payment that is worthy enough to reconcile us to God the Father once and for all, and that is the blood sacrifice that was offered on the cross at Calvary by Jesus Himself. The death, burial and resurrection of Christ is the good news that saves a man from eternal condemnation if you choose to believe it. But if you honestly believe it, you will be changed and changed forever. At that moment of salvation, the Holy Spirit enters into your heart. After that point, every time a person tries to live according to the flesh, the Holy Spirit convicts them. Through the process of sanctification, a believer grows in his or her relationship with Jesus and walks stronger each day. No longer wanting to walk according to the ways of the world, the Christian seeks to live a life that is pleasing to God.

You see, in order to experience the rapture one day, we have to be like Enoch in Genesis. We actually have to walk with the Lord, and not with the world. The Apostle Paul reminds us, "But as he which hath called you is holy, so be ye holy in all manner of conversation; Because it is written, Be ye holy; for I am holy" (1 Peter 1:15-16). We must be holy (separate from the world) and walk by faith in Jesus. The Bible teaches us, "But without faith it is impossible to please him: for he that cometh to God must believe that he is, and that he is a rewarder of them that diligently seek him:" (Hebrews 11:6). Therefore, if we are not walking by faith in Jesus, we are walking in accordance with the world. That is the opposite of what God has called us to do. Enoch walked by faith and was caught up with God.

If we walk by faith, we too will be caught up with Jesus and forever shall be with the Lord. The walk is evident in our lives by the manner in which we live. Do we live to please God, or do we live to please our flesh? I strongly encourage you to put away the world, put off the old man, embrace Jesus today, repent of your sins, and truly believe in your heart that Jesus has saved you from sin by his finished work on the Cross at Calvary. Then allow the Holy Spirit to work in your life. Be blessed and walk by faith.

- **Read Hebrews 11:5-6, Genesis 5:24, 1 Thessalonians 4:13-18, Colossians 3:8-9, Romans 3:23, & 1 Peter 1:15-16**
- Are you walking by faith in Jesus?
  - o Have you laid down the things of the world?
- How has your walk with the Lord changed your life?
  - o Are your friends the same as before?
- Has your walk in faith impacted anyone around you for the glory of God?
- Pray and continue to give God Thanks for the free gift of salvation and for using your walk to impact others for the glory of God.
- Log in your journal how your walk with Christ is impacting your relationship with others around you and how Christ has used your walk to lead others to the cross.

GOD IS THE JUDGE

There are many people in an uproar over the election this year. Of course, there were many people in an uproar over the past elections also. This country has been mostly divided down the middle since the turn of the century. Every election of the 21st century has been hotly contested with the exception of 2012. It seems as though Americans are at an impasse. Nearly half of the country wants to lean left and the other half leans right. Both sides bicker, fight, and fuss to the point where Americans are insulting one another and relationships between friends and family are broken, perhaps even beyond repair.

However, as Christians we are commanded to love one another by our Lord and Savior Jesus Christ. Regardless of someone's political stance, cultural upbringing, or any other categorical alliance, we are to love one another. Jesus says, "If ye love me, keep my commandments:" (John 14:15). When a certain Lawyer of the Pharisees asked Jesus which was the greatest commandment, Jesus replied, "…Thou shalt love the Lord thy God with all thy heart, and with all thy soul, and with all thy mind. This is the first and great commandment. And the second is like unto it, Thou shalt love thy neighbour as thyself. On these two commandments hang all the law and the prophets" (Matthew 22:37-40). And of course, we know that everyone is our neighbor. Even those we disagree with. Even those who do not believe the way we believe. Even those who oppose Christianity. Everyone is our neighbor.

Christians have an obligation to be involved in our political system and to vote according to the Word of God. The only way to know God's Will is to study His Word daily and commune with Him daily in prayer. We should seek to please God, not our own self-indulgence. And while it is true many today, even Christians, tend to vote for whichever candidate will help them the most financially or through social programs, we all need to be careful in this regard. We should study the candidates and vote for the ones who most closely resemble, preserve, protect, and defend our faith as outlined in the Bible. Notice, I did not say the candidate that was perfect, or the candidate that would save us from despair. There is only One who saves, and that is our Lord Jesus Christ. We should not ever put any candidate or elected official on a pedestal that exalts him over our Lord. Nor should we be drawn into an argument over which candidate resembles Christ. I have yet to see one.

While I hope and pray that people will continue to grow in their walk with Christ daily, study His Word, and seek to do His will above all else, I also understand the God is in complete control of every situation that we find ourselves. Even in 2020 with the pandemic, and election fraud claims, and bitterness between the left and right. Even in 2020 with riots involving Antifa and BLM and racial tension is at an all-time high, God is still on the Throne and He is still in control. His Word tells us, "For promotion cometh neither from the east, nor from the west, nor from the south. But God is the judge: he putteth down one, and setteth up another" (Psalm 76:6-7). Read that again. God is the judge, and it is He that puts one down and sets up another.

Let us not think too highly of ourselves. We are vessels that should be seeking to do God's Will daily. We are the clay, and He is the potter. God has a plan from start to finish that includes every one of us and this year is part of God's plan. It is understandable to be upset when we see things that we know are leaning towards evil. It is understandable to be upset when we see things happening that we know takes away from the Word of God. We should be distraught over this. But we should go to the Lord in prayer and supplication and continue to exalt our Lord Jesus Christ and preach the Gospel to everyone. We should continue to live our lives in a manner that is pleasing unto our Lord. But rather than be upset with our neighbor over the wickedness that we see, ask this question; how did we get here? The answer is that we, the church, have allowed us to get to this point.

We failed to raise up the generations behind us in the admonition of the Lord. We failed to instill the Word of God in our children and raise them by Biblical principles. We allowed the government to take God out of our schools and courthouses and have separated our lifestyle from

God. We are the ones who quit being Holy. Then we get upset because all of this is happening. We shout put God back in our schools and put God back in our courthouses. Yet, most have not even put God back in their homes. And there is the problem. We are where we are because we turned our back on Christ and His commandments.

Perhaps now, more than ever, we Christians need to start living the life that Jesus intends for us to live. Now is the time that we put Jesus first in our own lives, in our own homes, and make Him the center of our daily activities. Just maybe, if Christians loved God with all their heart, soul, and mind, and sought to make our lives a living sacrifice unto Him, and we loved our neighbor as ourselves, God would restore this country to prominence for His glory. However, if we fail to do so, we will surely go the way of ancient Israel and lose our nation altogether. And it will be deservedly so. But rather than being bitter at our neighbor and fighting amongst ourselves, let us examine our own life. Let us look in the mirror at how we are living. And remember this; it is God who is the judge, not man. It is God who sets one up and puts another down. And God is the righteous judge.

- **Read Psalm 76:6-7, Daniel 2:20-22, Romans 13:1-2 Matthew 22:37-40 and John 14:15**
- Do you get excited over politics and become fearful?
- Do you believe God is in control?
- The Bible says He is, so I encourage you to give it all to God and remain calm.
- This week pray that God will not only provide you with peace, but that His peace will be with everyone that calls upon His Holy name in faith.
- Write I your journal any observations you may have noticed either now or in the past where even Christians got upset over the political environment.
- How did they behave, and did you think that is the Christian thing to do?
- How can we make a difference?

OBEDIENCE IS BETTER THAN SACRIFICE

The Bible tells us, "For the word of God is quick, and powerful, and sharper than any twoedged sword, piercing even to the dividing asunder of soul and spirit, and of the joints and marrow, and is a discerner of the thoughts and intents of the heart" (Hebrews 4:12). Indeed, it is. God has preserved His Word for all people and for all times. The scriptures also let us know that Jesus Christ is the same yesterday, today, and forever (See Hebrews 13:8). Yet, in today's society we have grown accustomed to our current cancel culture mentality and like to remove anything that might offend anyone for any reason. But the Word of God does not change simply because the calendar does, or because someone does not like what it says. The Bible is the divinely inspired, infallible, inerrant Word of God and just like God himself, the Word does not change.

However, today Christianity has become an in vogue social club where people like to interject their thoughts, expressions and takes on what it means to be a Christian. I have actually heard people speak directly to me telling me that "their take" is that Jesus would or would not do something today because Jesus is love. And while I will agree that Jesus is love, someone else's "take" on who Jesus is or what Jesus would or would not do is irrelevant. I am not interested in any person's "take" on Jesus or the Bible. I am interested in the Truth as it is presented in the Bible, and that is what everyone else should be interested in as well. Simply telling people that Jesus loves them and that it is ok to continue to live a lifestyle of sin is an erroneous expression of the gospel and it will lead many to eternal damnation.

The Bible tells us plainly that obedience is better than sacrifice in 1 Samuel 15:22. God wants us to be obedient unto Him. That is why we have the Bible in the first place; so that we will know the gospel, believe in and on the name of Jesus, and understand what God expects from us. The Word of God tells us how to be saved, how to worship, when to assemble, how to conduct ourselves in our everyday lives and what to expect in the future for those who believe and for those who do not. The original sin in the garden of Eden that led to death for humanity was due to disobedience to God's direction for Adam and Eve. The flood was a direct consequence of humanity's continued disobedience. Israel and Judah being led back into captivity at the hands of Assyria and Babylon was due to direct disobedience and rebellion to God's Word.

Yet, somehow today, the modern Christian thinks that it does not matter how we live our lives. We just simply say a prayer and say we believe in Jesus, and we are saved and therefore we can continue to live as we always have. We can continue to be disobedient and there are no consequences we face. Well, regardless of anyone's "take" on this, that is not what the Bible teaches. Furthermore, the word "believe" needs to be examined deeply in one's heart. Because believing that Jesus is who He is requires obedience. The devil and his demons know who Jesus is, but they do not believe on His name and in His finished works on the cross at calvary. There are many people who "know" Jesus, yet deny his deity, grace, mercy, and love by the manner in which they live their lives. Many say they believe but fall short of living out their faith.

The Apostle Paul says it best in the book of Romans. "Know ye not, that to whom ye yield yourselves servants to obey, his servants ye are to whom ye obey; whether of sin unto death, or of obedience unto righteousness" (Romans 6:16)? You and I are servants. We are either servants of God through our faith in Jesus, or we are servants of the world. You and I get to choose each day who we serve. We are faced with the same question that Adam and Eve faced in Eden regarding the tree of the knowledge of good and evil. Are we going to partake of what God says or what the world says? Are we going to follow the commandments of the world or of God? The evidence of who we serve is obvious in the manner in which we live our daily lives.

It is also important to remember Galatians 6:7, "Be not deceived; God is not mocked: for whatsoever a man soweth, that shall he also reap." We are not fooling anyone. Who we say we are should be in line with how we live. Jesus tells us, "Strive to enter in at the strait gate: for many, I say unto you, will seek to enter in, and shall not be able"

(Luke 13:24). There are only two people who know your heart, you and the Lord Jesus Himself. However, it is imperative that we as Christians understand who we are in Christ and be obedient unto the Lord even as He was obedient unto the cross. There is no giving of money, charity, or any other substitute that takes the place of an obedient child of God. As His Word tells us, obedience is better than sacrifice.

- **Read 1 Samuel 15:22, Psalms 12:6-7, Romans 6:16, Galatians 6:7 & Hebrews 4:12 & 13:8**
- How have you grown in obedience to God's Word?
- Do you know professing Christians who are still "babes in Christ" and have not grown in their relationship?
- Do they rebel against obedience?
- How can you help those people in your lives grow in obedience in their walk with the Lord?
- Pray for God to touch the lives of every believer that they may walk in obedience to His Word. And pray that God would use you to help others grow in their relationship with Christ through obedience.
- Record in your journal any observations you make with your own walk and the walk of other Christians regarding obedience to His Word.

WISEMEN COME TO
WORSHIP JESUS

The Old Testament scriptures long prophesied of the birth of the Messiah. The savior of the world would be born in Bethlehem to a virgin and this baby boy would be called Emanuel, meaning God with us. However, when Jesus was born there were not a lot of people looking for a baby boy born in a manger. The Bible does tell us that wisemen from the east came to Jerusalem after seeing the star. Matthew 2:2 says that they came to worship Him. How amazing is that? Wisemen coming from a far land in the east to the Holy Land that was governed by an insanely jealous King Herod, to worship a baby they knew was born King of the Jews.

These wisemen risked a lot to travel across the desert into a land where they could possibly lose their life at the hands of King Herod, just so they could bring gifts to Jesus and worship the Son of God. King Herod actually caught wind of this and called the wisemen to himself in an attempt to get them to find Jesus and tell him where he was. Herod said it was so he could worship him also, but the wisemen knew it was not so. After following the star that went before them and finding Jesus, they were warned by God not to return to Herod. So, the wisemen departed another way to return home after presenting Jesus with gifts of frankincense, gold, and myrrh.

Bible scholars agree that the wisemen from the east were from across the desert some three hundred miles or more. Imagine traveling three hundred miles across a treacherous wilderness of dry barren land on foot, or camel or mule to worship God. And doing so knowing that you are entering a land in which you may even lose your life. Many people today cannot fathom that type of devotion. Many today will not travel 3 miles to get to their local church to worship God, let alone travel 300 miles across dangerous land in the face of what could be sheer death to worship God. But that is the difference between those who seek God and those who do not.

There is a passage of scripture from the prophet Jeremiah that I believe God uses to prick the hearts of men and women. He first used it to get the attention of the Jews, but the passage applies to believers in Christ even today. God says through the prophet, "And ye shall seek me, and find me, when ye shall search for me with all your heart" (Jeremiah 29:13). It is obvious that the wisemen sought God with their whole heart. They didn't just say they were seeking him, they showed they were seeking him. Against all odds the wisemen sought to find Jesus. My question to the readers today and to those around you is, are you seeking Jesus with your whole heart? Jesus isn't hiding and he isn't dead. He is as alive today as He has been for all eternity. Nobody has to travel hundreds of miles across desert terrain to locate Him either. He is right there beside you just waiting for you to call upon Him.

Once you have called upon Him, repented from your sins, believe in and on the name of Jesus, and confess Jesus is the Son of God, you are saved forever. The Holy Spirit comes into your heart that instant and will guide you, convict you, and teach you by giving you wisdom and understanding of His Holy Word in the Bible. As a born-again believer in Christ, you worship the Lord in the manner in which you now live for him, putting off your old self and your old ways, and putting on the new person in Christ Jesus. We do this so that Jesus can be seen in us and be glorified through us, so that others can come to know Jesus and have the free gift of salvation.

This Christmas season let us not forget that we are celebrating the birth of our Lord and Savior, Jesus Christ. The greatest Christmas gift of all time is salvation by the grace of our God through faith in His only begotten Son. If you are born-again then continue to worship King Jesus in the manner in which you live your life. We don't have to travel 300 miles. We can do it right where we live, and we should be doing it daily. Make sure you are telling someone else about Jesus also and let them know that the wise still seek Him.

- **Read Jermiah 29:13, Matthew 2:1-12 & Matthew 5:16**
- How does the story of the wisemen traveling to find Jesus affect you spiritually?

- Are you willing to travel and risk your life to worship the Lord?
  - Some Christians are not willing to go to Church when it is raining.
- Do you show your worship of Christ in your life everyday right where you are?
  - Are you glorifying our Father in Heaven by your daily worship?
- Continue to pray with thanksgiving that God will use your daily worship as a witness for Him and that others may come to salvation through your witness.
- Write in your daily journal about your daily walk as you remember the wisemen's travel from afar to get to Jesus.

A RESOLUTION WORTH KEEPING

Many people still make new year's resolutions. Although some resolve that they won't make any resolutions at all, mainly because they know in their heart that they won't be able to keep them. But what exactly is a resolution to begin with? To have resolve is to have fixity or a purpose according to Merriam-Webster. That is to say that you have made up your mind to stick with something. Whatever it may be, you are going to see it through to fruition regardless of the circumstances. Some people make new year's resolutions to lose weight, or to get into shape. While these are both good resolutions to have, I think we forget about the most important resolution that anyone can ever make.

As a born-again Christian, we have made a covenant with God to put our faith in Jesus Christ as the only begotten Son of God who came into this world and willingly laid down His life for our sins, so that we may everlasting life. That covenant between God and us declares that God gives us ever-lasting life and we state that we will surrender our lives unto Him and live a life that is pleasing unto God. But of course, we don't do it alone. We have the Holy Spirit living inside us to convict us and guide us in our daily lives. Yet many people tend to resort back to the fleshly way of living over time, ignoring the convictions of the Holy Spirit and following after the worldly lusts that we surround ourselves with.

The Lord says, "A new heart also will I give you, and a new spirit will I put within you: and I will take away the stony heart out of your flesh, and I will give you an heart of flesh" (Ezekiel 36:26). When we first come to Christ we become "on fire" for the Lord, but many begin to fade over time. Rather than continuing to lean on the Holy Spirit and His wisdom and guidance some turn back to the world. With regard to that the Bible tells us, "Let no man deceive himself. If any man among you seemeth to be wise in this world, let him become a fool, that he may be wise. For the wisdom of this world is foolishness with God. For it is written, He taketh the wise in their own craftiness" (1 Corinthians 3:18-19).

The Lord warns us throughout the Bible not to give in to the sins of this world and the lies that the devil uses to deceive us. However, people tend to turn back to what their friends are doing in an attempt to appease the world and their flesh. After publicly accepting Jesus as Lord and Savior, committing their lives to the Lord, they return to the filth in which Jesus cleansed them from. This should not be. It is important to point out that salvation through faith in Christ is not a social club membership. The Bible says we are bought with a price and are to glorify Christ (see 1 Corinthians 6:20 and 7:23). And it is also equally important to remind everyone, "Be not deceived; God is not mocked: for whatsoever a man soweth, that shall he also reap" (Galatians 6:7).

As the year ends and we turn the page of the calendar to a new year, let us make a resolution that is worth keeping. Let us be resolute in our faith and deliberate in our walk with Jesus. Let us follow righteousness. "Fight the good fight of faith, lay hold on eternal life, whereunto thou art also called, and hast professed a good profession before many witnesses" (1 Timothy 6:12). Furthermore, let us have steadfast resolve daily. Before our feet hit the floor let us make a declaration to God to do His will and not our own; to die to self and live for Him.

- **Read Ezekiel 36:26, 1 Corinthians 6:20 & 7:23, Galatians 6:7 & 1 Timothy 6:12**
- Which wisdom are you seeking today?
- Wisdom of the world or the wisdom of God?
- Have you made resolutions and failed to keep them?
- As a reminder when we came to Christ in faith it was more than a resolution tat could be broken, it was a covenant that seals you to eternity.
- Pray that God will hold you close and accountable to the Gospel of Jesus and His Holy Word.

- Help others that you know are walking with the Lord as an accountability partner in Christ.
- Write down in your journal how God has reminded you of your faith walk with Christ and how He is using you with other believers in their walk as well.

IS IT TIME TO CLEANSE THE TEMPLE?

In 2 Chronicles Chapter 29, we read that King Hezekiah begins to reign in Judah. Verse two tells us that he did "right in the sight of the Lord." Hezekiah was the son of Ahaz who was a terribly evil king during his time. Ahaz had performed pagan practices in the temple and desecrated all that was sacred in the house of the Lord. During Ahaz's tenure as King of Judah his people turned away from serving God and turned toward idolatry. It is atypical to think that Ahaz could have a child that would be the opposite of his own characteristics. However, Hezekiah served the Lord, God Almighty.

King Hezekiah saw the evil that was going on around him as well as the evil that was occurring to Judah. He knew in his heart that the cause of the evil was due to Judah turning their backs toward God and serving themselves. As a result, the young Hezekiah ordered a cleansing of the temple and orchestrated a return to serving the God of all creation, the God of Abraham, Isaac, and Jacob. King Hezekiah said, "Now it is in mine heart to make a covenant with the LORD God of Israel, that his fierce wrath may turn away from us" (2 Chronicles 29:10). He tells his people not to be negligent, "for the Lord hath chosen you to stand before him, to serve him..." (2 Chronicles 29:11). In response to the call of Hezekiah, they cleansed and sanctified the house of the Lord.

The Bible says that King Hezekiah "did that which was right in the sight of the Lord" (2 Kings 18:3). He insured that all the pagan images were torn down and destroyed and served the Lord our God. The scripture tells us that there was never a king before or after him that was like he was. He clave to God and "the Lord was with him" (2 Kings 18:7). God was with Hezekiah wherever he went, and the Lord blessed him and Judah because of his attitude and service to

God. In fact, the Lord actually sent angels to deliver Judah out of the hands of Assyria who had surrounded them. The angles destroyed 185,000 Assyrians that were encamped round Judah. These are the same Assyrians that earlier had taken Samaria from the northern kingdom of Israel.

It is no secret that God blesses those who serve Him. The Hebrew people were called by God as his own chosen people, and He gave them commandments and instructions for how to live. When they served Him and obeyed His commandments, He blessed them. However, when they turned from walking with the Lord, they faced the consequences of such an action. And whatever God did or allowed to happen to them, he did so in order that they may know that He is God and return to Him. The Bible tells us clearly, "For whom the Lord loveth he chasteneth, and scourgeth every son whom he receiveth" (Hebrews 12:6).

As Christians, we have the Holy Spirit of God living in us. Our Body has become the Temple of the Living God. Yet many people who call themselves Christians have quit serving the Lord and have turned their back on Him. A lot of professing believers in Christ have defiled the Temple just as the Jewish people did in King Ahaz's day. They have returned to serving their fleshly lusts and have exalted the idolatry of the day. If this is you, I implore you to cleanse the Temple. Ask for forgiveness and repent from the wickedness that is in this world. Return to serving the Lord our God through faith in Christ Jesus. Stand before Him and serve Him as His redeemed.

- **Read 2 Chronicles 29, 2 Kings 18:1-7 & Hebrews 12:6**
- Even though we are not kings of a nation, we are rulers over our bodies, which is the Temple of God.
- How is your Temple today?
  - o Are you honoring God or the world?
- Do you know of any "Christians" that treat their Temple poorly?
  - o How does that make you feel?
- Pray that God would help everyone who professes Christ to live a God honoring life, keeping their Temple clean and being a strong witness for the Lord.

- Pray also that God will use you as an example for others to follow as you follow Christ and His Word.
- Journal anything you have witnessed regarding yourself or other Christians honoring or dishonoring God with their bodies and express how that influences you moving forward.

WORRY LESS, TRUST MORE

"Which of you by taking thought can add one cubit unto his stature" (Matthew 6:27)? This is the question that our Lord Jesus poses to us. Today more than ever we have and overabundance of worrywarts in our society. People worry about everything from how they will pay bills all the way down to which shoes to wear today. If there is a topic, someone somewhere is worried about it. Worry does nothing but make the population anxious. And of course, the Bible tells us to "Be careful for nothing; but in everything by prayer and supplication with thanksgiving let your requests be made known unto God" (Philippians 4:6). Yet we tend to take on the troublesome task of concerning ourselves with every apprehension of the world as if it is our job to take care of it all.

As Christians we are not supposed to live in that manner. We are supposed to live by faith and not by sight and have the peace of the Lord within us (see Romans 5:1-2). In Matthew chapter six verses 25-34, the Lord Jesus makes it clear that we should not worry about the things of this life. He uses the birds as an example, because they do not reap or sow, yet God takes care of them and provides for their every need. Then He illustrates to us that the lilies in the fields grow beautifully without doing one thing to earn their splendor. And Jesus magnifies our importance to God the Father by telling us that we are greater than the birds of the sky or the grass in the field.

As a preacher I like to ask questions of followers of Christ. One of the most important questions I could ever ask is this; do you believe every word of the Bible? Your answer will determine the amount of anxiety you have in life. I know the Holy Bible is the infallible, inerrant, divinely inspired Word of God, and therefore it is the Truth given to us by our Heavenly Father. God cannot lie. In His Word, we are told to give it to God and let Him deal with it. "It" is any and everything you worry about! You may be in a situation today where you are concerned with how you will pay your rent or mortgage, how you will get groceries for your family so your children can eat, or myriads of things that will consume your emotions. These worries are placed in front of you by the great deceiver, the devil. Worry is a tool used by Satan to destroy your relationship with God.

Jesus tells us to take no thought what we will eat, or drink or what we will wear because God is well aware that we have needs (Matthew 6:31-32). So how do we just let go and let God take care of us without worrying about everything? It is simple. We do what God tells us to do in His Holy Word. He tells us, "But seek ye first the kingdom of God, and his righteousness and all these things will be added unto you" (Matthew 6:33). So, the questions now become; are we seeking God first in our lives? Are we looking to live a righteous life in accordance with His Word? Are we looking to live a pleasing life unto God? Have we accepted Jesus as Lord and savior and put off the old man and put on the new? Are we fully trusting God to do what He said He will do?

Remember, God cannot lie. He tells us we are greater than the birds of the sky and the grass of the fields which He feeds and clothes. Then He tells us that if we seek Him first, He will provide everything we need without worry. Perhaps we should stop allowing the devil to dictate our lives, and we start blossoming into that which God has created us to be by committing ourselves to Him. By doing so we can remove worry and anxiety from our lives and be joyful in the Lord knowing that He is going to take care of us just like He said.

- **Read Matthew 6:25-34, Philippians 4:6 & Romans 5:1-2**
- Are you a worrywart?
  - o I pray that you give your worries to the Lord and let Him deal with them.
  - o Remember if we do the things God tells us to do, He will perform the things He tells us He will.
  - o Seek Him with your whole heart. He'll take care of you.
- Pray for the Lord to strengthen you in your faith knowing that He will provide for you.

o You are much more than the birds of the air or grass in a field. You are His child.

- Record in your journal how God has taken care of things in times past and give God all glory for the great things He has done. And even thank Him and praise Him for the things he already has planned for you that you do not even know about yet.

WEEK FIFTY
STRANGE THINGS TO THE EARS

If you listen to mainstream radio or even watch a great deal of television, you will inevitably hear some pretty strange things. I have even heard some pretty strange things in the grocery store checkout line. The things that come out of people's mouths today astonish me. Not only is there no filter involved, but there is also no respect given to the general public gathered around. The vulgar conversation and disgusting topics that people just accept as the norm is alarming. People generally believe that since they talk that way then everyone else must talk that way. Or perhaps they really don't care if anyone else talks that way, they are just going to speak whatever they desire without regard to their surroundings.

Unfortunately, these words and topics are not so strange to my ears anymore. They have become the norm in our society. They are a celebration of the abomination of the tongue. But the thing that has become strange to the ears is the gospel of Jesus Christ being spoken in public. Apparently, it is ok to speak the good news in churches, and Bible studies but not in the market checkout line. I have seen more disgusted faces and eyes rolling over the dialogue of Jesus than I have over the use of curse words in public in the latter years. How far we have fallen O' America.

In the book of Acts we come to a story where Paul is in Athens preaching the gospel of Jesus Christ in chapter 17. Verse 16 says that his spirit was stirred in him because he saw the city was given to idolatry. The scripture goes on to say that philosophers were concerned with what he was speaking, "for thou bringest certain strange things to our ears: we would know therefore what these things mean" (Acts 17:20). I can only pray that today our spirits would be stirred and moved to the point of speaking out against the sin of our current society and speaking up for Jesus and His coming Kingdom. If we as Christians would do as the Lord has commanded us and preach the gospel to every creature (see Mark 16:15), then perhaps the people would listen and desire to know what these things actually mean.

How sad is it that speaking the gospel of Jesus Christ has become strange things to the ears of the residents of our communities? How sad is it that cursing and speaking filthily has become the accepted standard conversation in public, but speaking the truth in Christ Jesus has become off-limits. If only the body of Christ would boldly proclaim the Word of God and do so in routine speech, perhaps the national conversation would turn from filth to godliness and praiseworthy dialog. Why are we allowing Satan to dictate our conversation? At one time in our country, speaking about our Lord and Savior and church, and sharing the gospel was not only the norm, but it was also part of the national culture. And in just a few short generations we have come to the point where we can't mention the name of Jesus without a revolting look from bystanders.

As a preacher of the Word of God and presenter of the gospel of Jesus Christ I say it is past time to return our society back to the Lord. Just as speaking about last night's ball game is common speak and discussing the current prices of gasoline is a conversation piece, we need to be speaking of the good news of the saving grace of God through faith in Jesus Christ. Moreover, we should be filling the ears of the public with the Word that can save a soul rather than speaking words that only tickle the ears of the hearer and offend the Spirit. As followers of Jesus Christ and doers of the Word (see James 1:22), let us put strange things back in the ears of every listener within earshot. As Paul was stirred by the spirit, I pray that we all will be so moved. The gospel sounds strange to the sinner who hasn't heard the truth. But the truth can set them free and if it is accepted, then they will share in the eternal life that we now have.

- **Read Acts Chapter 17, Mark 16:15 & James 1:22**
- As you have read, God did some amazing things through the Apostle Paul because he opened his mouth in public.
    - Do you think God can and will do similar things through your conversation?
- When was the last time you spoke about Jesus publicly?

- o Not even sharing the Gospel, just talking to someone openly in public about Jesus and what He has done for you.
- Pary that God would not only use you, but use other Christians to return our public squares, grocery stores and other meeting places into a forum to discuss Christ openly.
  - o Pray that God will make it common again to speak of our Lord and Savior.
- Make a journal entry about your observations of Christ being publicly spoken about.
  - o Record how He was being spoken of, and the reaction that the conversation received.

BELIEVER'S BAPTISM

The subject of baptism in the church has become a topic of discussion and even dispute among many. There are priests, and pastors of some denominations that preach and teach infant baptism and christening. Christening has become a rather large ceremonial tradition with the Catholic church and with some denominations of reformed churches that splintered out of Catholicism. These ceremonies usually take place when the child is an infant. Parents present their children in front of the church where they are baptized (christened) and often times given a new name that is biblical in origin. They are also often presented with a set of godparents who are chosen by the biological parents to help raise and guide the children through life in godliness (Sanchez, 2022). While this ritual appears to be a righteous act on the part of the parents to raise their children up in the church, it is not biblical in any manner.

As Christians, followers of Christ, we surrender to His authority and His Word as our guidance and instruction for living while we are on earth. Regardless of how good the intentions are by the parents and the churches, infant baptism, and/or christening, is not found anywhere in the Bible (I challenge the reader to search the scriptures for this subject). There is no ritual, instruction, command, or suggestion that would even give the slightest inclination that this event should take place. Since the Bible is a Christian's final and only authority, there is no need to consult another book or manual to find such a ritual to perform. And if the Bible is not the authority in which a church operates, then that church is not a church belonging to the Body of Christ. The church that deviates from the Bible has deviated from God's Word, and therefore has deviated from God.

The Bible teaches believer's baptism. One particular story in the book of Acts stands out to me. In Acts 8:26-38 we find the account of the eunuch of Ethiopia who was passing through Gaza to go and worship. He was reading scripture from the prophet Isaiah when the Spirit of the Lord spoke to the Apostle Phillip to go and speak with him. Phillip climbed on the chariot in which the eunuch was riding and inquired if the eunuch understood the words he was reading. The eunuch said he couldn't unless someone explained them to him. He was reading what we know as Isaiah 53:7-8 today and asked Phillip if the scripture was referring to Isaiah himself, or another man. "Then Phillip opened his mouth and began at the same scripture and preached unto him Jesus" (Acts 8:35).

They came to a certain water body and the eunuch said to Phillip, "See here is water: what doth hinder me to be baptized" (Acts 8:36)? Phillip's response is the most significant point about what is required for baptism. "And Phillip said, if thou believest with all thine heart, thou mayest. And he answered and said, I believe that Jesus is the Son of God" (Acts 8:37). Based on the eunuch's response, the chariot was halted, and they went down to the water where Phillip baptized him. This account in the Bible gives us the guidance needed for baptism.

In order to be baptized, one must believe in their heart that Jesus is the Son of God; that He is the Messiah. We must believe that Jesus was born of a virgin, lived a sinless life, willingly bled, and laid down his life on the cross at Calvary. We must believe that He was crucified, dead, and buried and rose again from the grave on the third day and that He ascended into heaven and sits at the Father's right hand today making intercession for us. We must believe that Jesus will one day soon return and call his bride, the church, home. The Bible tells us that this is who Jesus is, and this is what Jesus did, and this is what Jesus will do. If a person believes this and confesses with their mouth, then they are saved for all eternity (see Romans 10:9 and 1 John 4:15).

Baptism is an outward show of someone's inner faith in Jesus Christ as Lord and Savior. Therefore, in order to be baptized a person must believe in Jesus Christ and that He is who the Bible says He is; the Son of God, God incarnate, the Messiah, the Lamb of God who takes away the sins of the world. An infant or child who cannot communicate or who is not of the age of accountability, cannot confess nor can he or she accept Jesus in faith. They cannot accept what they do not know or understand. We, as parents, are instructed to raise our children up in righteousness (see proverbs 22:6) so that they will come to the knowledge of Christ and accept Him freely for themselves.

As much as we want to save our children, ultimately the free gift of the saving grace of God by faith in Jesus Christ has to be received by each individual. Our children are included in that. We cannot save them by christening them or baptizing them at birth or at an immature age. They must be of understanding and knowledge and accept Christ for themselves. If we are really interested in saving our children from eternal condemnation after this life, we will raise them up in the admonition of the Lord, teaching them the scriptures, and ensuring they are raised in church and around other believers in Christ. This is the mark of a Godly parent. Let us follow the Word of God in truth and not the rituals of man. Following man will lead to hell, following God and His Word leads to eternal glory.

- **Read Acts 8:26-38, Romans 10:9-10&13, 1 John 4:15 and Proverbs 22:6**
- Do believe it is important to follow the Word of God rather than rituals of man?
- What are the dangers of not following the Bible?
    - o Do you think it is possible for someone to think they are saved because they were Christened or baptized at a young age?
    - o Were you able to find any scriptures about infant baptism or christening anywhere in the Bible?
- Pray for believers everywhere to be led by the scriptures in the Holy Bible and not by man's traditions.
    - o If you know of someone who was christened or baptized at a young age, ask them about their salvation and make sure they have placed their faith and trust in Jesus and are not relying on those "works".
- Journal your thoughts on what we discussed and what the scriptures state regarding baptism.

WHAT IS SALVATION?

The most important thing in the ministry is the salvation of the sinner. It is easy to become engrossed with the many sides of serving the Lord; preparing for Sunday school, writing sermons, drafting an article for the paper, calling, or visiting the congregation, officiating funerals and weddings, and the list goes on and on. However, the most important part of serving the Lord is spreading the gospel of Jesus Christ so that others may receive Jesus as their Lord and Savior and be saved. In reviewing these articles for this book, it became clear to me that I have given a clear presentation of the good news of the saving grace of God through Jesus Christ, His only begotten Son. It is easy for me to assume you are saved because you bought this devotional, but I want to make sure.

The first thing I want everyone to understand is that Salvation is not a plan that you put into place and work toward. There is not a step process that you follow to be saved from eternal condemnation. You cannot work to be saved. The Bible says, "For by grace are ye saved through faith; and that not of yourselves: it is the gift of God: Not of works, lest any man should boast" (Ephesians 2:8-9). Pastor Adrian Rodgers once said quite simply, "salivation is not a plan, it is a man" (Rogers, n.d.). The man we speak of is Jesus Christ. He is both fully man and fully God.

Jesus is the second person of the triune God; God the Father, God the Son, and God the Holy Spirit. And as Jesus himself said, He is the only way for salvation, there is no other way. "Jesus saith unto him, I am the way, the truth, and the life: no man cometh unto the Father, but by me" (John 14:6). There isn't any other way regardless of what the world may tell you. There aren't many paths to heaven, there is only one. God's free gift to humanity is his Son Jesus as the only sacrifice for the sins of man. Jesus is the perfect lamb of God which takes away the sins of the world. But you have to receive him freely by your will and desire. He will not force himself upon you and will not save you without you asking him to do so personally.

You might be thinking, I am a good person, and I don't need saving. Or perhaps you think you do not sin. The Bible tells us, there is "none that doeth good" (see Psalm 14:3), and the Apostle Paul tells us, "For all have sinned, and come short of the glory of God;" (Romans 3:23). In God's eyes we have all sinned and come short of his glory. We are born into the sinful world and desire to sin against God and have been this way since the fall of man in the garden of Eden. Because Adam rebelled against God and did according to his own desire, death entered into the world. "Wherefore, as by one man sin entered into the world, and death by sin; and so death passed upon all men, for that all have sinned:" (Romans 5:12). Without salvation all of human creation is on a path to death and hell. Because the Bible tells us the wages of sin is death (see Romans 6:23).

Now you might be thinking that this is all a hopeless cause and that we are all doomed because nobody can live up to the glory of God. Here is where the "good news" comes in. The Gospel is the saving grace of God through faith in Jesus Christ. God gave us all a way out of death and hell when Jesus willingly laid down his life on the cross on Calvary's hill. Jesus, God incarnate, lived a sinless and perfect life on earth, and sacrificed his life for our sins. Romans 5:8 tells us that "while we yet sinners, Christ died for us." He was dead and buried in a tomb for three days and rose again from the grave (physically) and ascended into heaven, where he sits at the right hand of the Father making intercession for believers today. And one day soon, He is coming back to call his bride (The Church) home to escape the wrath to come. This is the Gospel, the Good News of the death, burial resurrection of our Lord and savior Jesus Christ (see 1 Corinthians 15:1-4). And what a wonderful underserving blessing God has provided for us all, if only we all would receive it.

So, how does one become saved and receive the free gift of salvation? What must a person do to be saved? Well, just as God tells us in His Word, we don't have to earn it. We could never earn our way into heaven. We could never do enough good work to warrant forgiveness of our sins. God gives it to us freely as long as we freely receive it. The Bible says, "That if thou shalt confess with thy mouth the Lord Jesus, and shalt believe in thine heart that God hath raised him from the dead, thou shalt be saved" (Romans 10:9). Simply put, call out to Jesus in prayer, and ask him to save you. Tell God that you know you are a sinner and deserving of death, but you believe Jesus is the Son of the living God, and that Jesus died for your sins. Tell Jesus that you receive Him as your personal Lord and Savior. If you pray a simple prayer such as this and mean it, He will save you and the Holy Spirit will enter into your heart.

My prayer for you, the reader, is that you have either received the free gift of salvation by faith in Jesus Christ, or you will do so now. For those who have received Jesus Christ and are saved for all eternity I pray that you be encouraged in the Spirit and share the Gospel with others. The day is fast approaching when the church will be called home. The rapture is imminent. Remember what Jesus said, "The harvest truly is great, but the labourers are few:" (Luke 10:2).

- **Read Romans 3:23, 5:12, 5:8, 6:23, 10:9-10&13, Ephesians 2:8-9 and 1 Corinthians 15:1-4**
- Are you saved?
- Are you sharing the good news with others?
- Pray that God would use you to share the Gospel so others can have the free gift of salvation through faith in Jesus.
- Journal how God is using you for His glory by sharing the Gospel message.

EPILOGUE/CONCLUSION

Congratulations on completing this fifty-two-week devotional. I truly hope that it was a blessing to you and that it helped you in your walk with the Lord. My goal in presenting this work was to get people to think and delve more into their Bibles for themselves. Nobody should ever blindly accept what anyone tells them regarding the Bible without examining God's Word themselves. We should all be as the Berean people in Acts chapter 17 and search the scriptures.

The Bible is the Holy, divinely inspired, inerrant, infallible and all sufficient Word of God. Nothing outside of the Bible should ever take the place of God's Word, not this writing or any other writing. All extrabiblical information that we consume should be done with an incredible amount of careful and prayerful discernment. I strongly believe the King James Bible is the Word for all English-Speaking people and has been the time-honored standard since its first publication in 1611. No other translation has touched my heart or changed my life the way His Book has. No other book, commentary, devotional, magazine, or pamphlet or any other literary work should be considered authoritative in nature outside of the Bible. We have God's Word, and it does not need fixing. It needs reading, it needs studying, and it needs applying!

I do so hope and pray that you received some level of blessing from this collection of articles that I have written based on God's Holy Word. I pray that it caused you to think, pray and examine the Word of God more closely than ever before. Even if you did not see "eye to eye" with my commentary on the topics presented, I pray that you drew closer to Christ through the Study of His Word. If it did anything to enrich your relationship with Jesus, I am thankful and bestow all Glory to God. I pray that you may be richly blessed in all your endeavors for the glory of God and that you move forward in this life spreading the Gospel of Jesus!

Because of Calvary,
Bro. Richie

BIBLIOGRAPHY

Bible Gateway. (2020). Retrieved from Bible Gateway: https://www. biblegateway.com/resources/encyclopedia-of-the-bible/Agape

King James Bible. (1611). Cambridge: Cambridge.

Koukol, G. (2013, February 28). *Stand to Reason: Faith of our Fathers.* Retrieved from str.org: https://www.str.org/w/the-faith-of-our-fathers

Lindsey, E. H. (n.d.). *He Made a Change.* Retrieved from lyricsondemand.com.

Online Dictionary. (2020). Retrieved from bing.com: https://www. bing.com/search?q=discernment&cvid=0c23343e99b74e7988 03f4a6fddb2096&gs_lcrp=EgZjaHJvbWUqBggAEAAYQDI GCAAQABhAMgYIARAuGEAyBggCEAAYQDIGCAMQA BhAMgYIBBAAGEAyBggFEAAYQDIGCAYQABhAMgY IBxBFGDwyBggIEEUYPNIBCDE5OTFqMGoxqAIAsAIA &FORM=ANAB01&PC=HCTS

Piper, J. (1986, February 9). *Blessed are the Meek.* Retrieved from desiringgod. org: https://www.desiringgod.org/messages/blessed-are-the-meek

Rogers, A. (n.d.). *Love Worth Finding.* Retrieved from Love worth Finding: https://www.lwf.org/

Sanchez, L. (2022, march 29). *Crosswalk.com.* Retrieved from Crosswalk,com: https://www.crosswalk.com/family/parenting/ new-parents/what-is-christening.html

Sandoiu, A. (2020, May 11). *COVID-19:3-drug combo treatment may be successful.* Retrieved from medicalnewstoday.com: https:// www.medicalnewstoday.com/articles/covid-19-3-drug-combo- treatment-may-be-successful

Smith, S. (2020). *Spencer Smith.* Retrieved from YouTube: https://www. youtube.com/@spencersmith312

Webster. (2020). *webster.com.* Retrieved from merria-Webster Dictionary: https://www.merriam-webster.com/dictionary/charity

ACKNOWLEDGMENTS

All Glory, Honor and Praise to God the Father. For by His Grace am I saved by faith in and of my Lord and Savior Jesus Christ and His finished work of the death, burial, and resurrection. I am humbled by the high calling You have placed on my life, and even though I am unworthy of the gifts and blessings from You, I am so extremely grateful and pray that I am useful to You, O Lord until you call me home. In Jesus' name – Amen.

I would like to thank my wife Sara once again for all of her love and support. Without her I could not be who I am. I would also like to thank Kevin and Becky Cox for all their love and support. Everybody should have good and faithful Christian friends as you two have been to Sara and me. Thanks to Brother Bryan Cox, who has shared hours upon hours of telephone conversation with me regarding the Bible and the problems we as Christians face today in our society. Thanks also to Chris Danley, Travis and Kirstie Haines, Jeff and Laurie Kresch, Bubba and Michele Jacobs, The Barker family (that is about half of the church), Amos and Kaye Dawley, Michelle and Gregg Smith, Charlie and Jeannie Nichols, Dave and Marcy Cunningham, Arthur and Roberta Jacobs, Dave and June Ovitt, Charlotte Thompson and the entire Word of Faith Bible Church family.

A special thank you to my musically gifted and wonderful friends Barbara Cox, Roe Copper and Becky Cox. The hymns and songs of praise that we sing in our church are made more beautiful by the backdrop of your instruments. Not only am I spiritually motivated, but our church is encouraged, and God is honored, glorified and praised through your wonderful music. With Brother Kevin leading the singing and you three providing the music each week, our small Church sounds as loud and as strong as any Mega-Church choir. And though I may be a tad bit biased, I must say we just sound better!

ABOUT THE AUTHOR

Richard (Richie) Thomas is an ordained minister of the Gospel of Jesus Christ, who served as the associate pastor under Pastor Howard Cox at Word of Faith Bible Church in Crescent City, Florida from February 2018 to February 2023. He was elected and installed as only the 3rd Pastor of Word of Faith Bible Church on 26 February 2023. Word of Faith Bible Church is an Independent, Fundamental, Evangelistic King James Bible preaching and teaching Church unaffiliated with the Charismatic "Word of Faith" movement. Brother Richie is a former Marine Corps Corporal (89-93) and U.S. Army Sergeant First Class (95-03) who also served as government contract employee and High School History teacher prior to his ordination.

Brother Richie will be the first to tell you that he has not always lived his life in accordance with the Bible. He is an imperfect man who lived a life of sin, experiencing failed relationships, self-inflicted hardships, and admittedly tried to justify his life by using the modernists excuses, "Jesus loves me no matter what" and "I am saved, so it doesn't matter what I do or how I live". It was only after Richie hit rock bottom in his life that he cried out to Jesus and began searching the scriptures for himself, leaning on the wisdom of the Holy Spirit through fervent prayer when he realized he was not living the life Christ died to give him. The book of Ecclesiasts and Paul's Letter to the Romans changed his life tremendously for the glory of God. He surrendered to the call into the ministry in 2017 and makes it his life's purpose to tell others the Truth in God's Word and encourage them to read it for themselves.

Pastor Richie holds a B.S. degree in Business Administration from Colorado Technical University, and a M.Ed. in Curriculum and Instruction with a focus on Social Studies from Concordia University. As an associate Pastor he was a weekly contributor to the 'Putnam County Courier Journal' writing the *Pastor's Pen* article from 2019 through 2021. He has been the guest preacher at other churches and addressed the inmates at Tomoka State Prison in Volusia County, Florida for "Revival Week" in 2022. He enjoys Gospel singing and plays the saxophone, guitar, bass and is learning piano. He and his wife Sara have five adult children and live in their hometown of Crescent City, Florida.